# PIECED
# Vegetables

## RUTH B. MCDOWELL

© 2002 Ruth B. McDowell

Developmental Editors: Karyn Hoyt, Barbara Konzak Kuhn
Technical Editor: Karyn Hoyt
Copy Editor: Lucy Grijalva
Design Director: Aliza Shalit
Book Design and Production: Aliza Shalit
Cover Design: Aliza Shalit
Production Assistant: Tim Manibusan
Illustrator: Kandy Petersen
Photographer: David Caras

Attention Teachers: C&T Publishing, Inc. encourages you to use this book as a text for teaching. Contact us at 800-284-1114 or www.ctpub.com for more information about the C&T Teachers Program.

**Library of Congress Cataloging-in-Publication Data**
McDowell, Ruth B.
   Pieced vegetables / Ruth B. McDowell.
      p. cm.
   Includes index.
   ISBN 1-57120-140-8 (paper trade)
   1. Patchwork--Patterns. 2. Patchwork quilts. 3. Vegetables in art.   I. Title.
TT835 .M2763 2002
746.46'041--dc21
                         2001005049

Published by C&T Publishing, Inc.
P.O. Box 1456
Lafayette, California 94549

Printed in China
10   9   8   7   6   5   4   3   2   1

To F.S. and M.E.

# contents

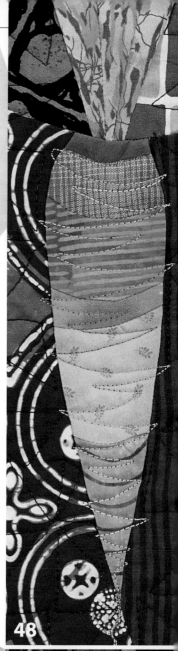

48

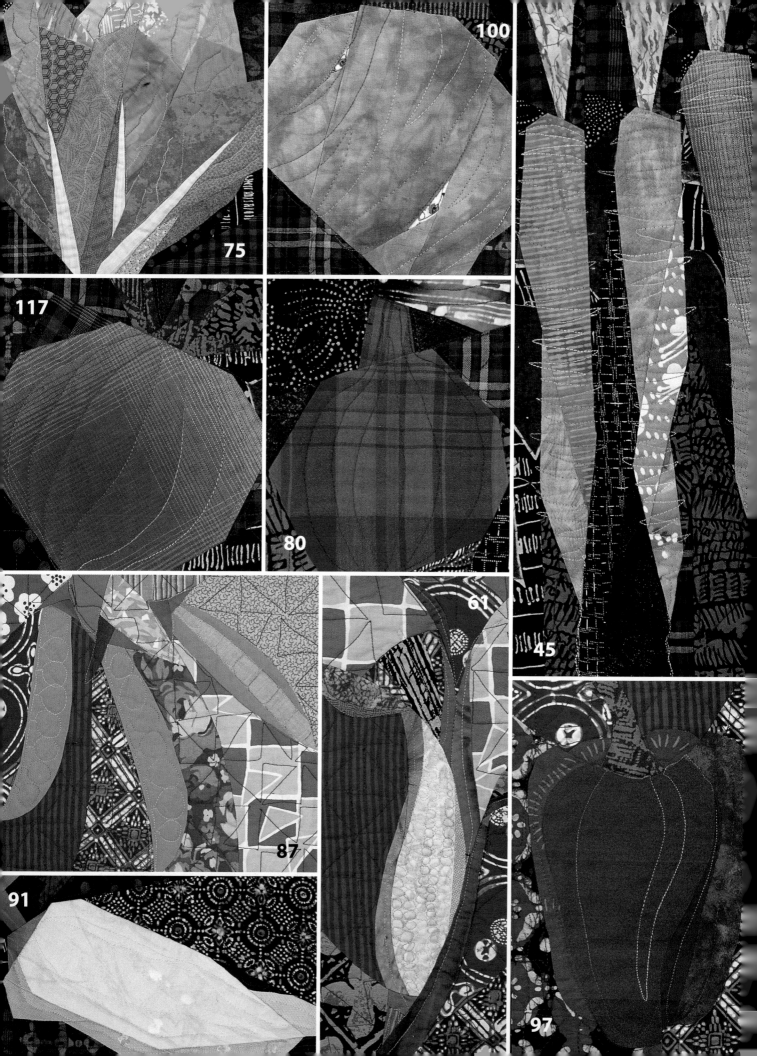

**30**

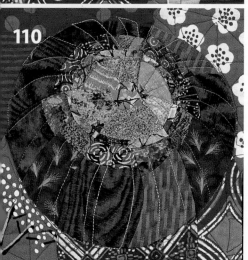

**110**

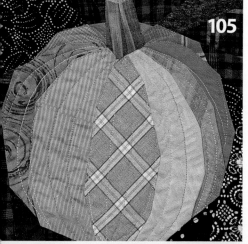

**105**

**39**

# INTRODUCTION

The shapes and colors of common vegetables are fascinating. They adapt very well to piecing, as the blocks in this book show. The blocks have been planned to be used either as repeated units, as illustrated in each chapter, or individually as placemats or small wall-hangings, or one of each block as a sampler quilt, as shown on pages 124 and 125.

# PIECING

All of the blocks in this book have been designed with several things in mind: first, the depiction of the vegetable subject; second, the relative ease of piecing; and third, the design possibilities for the overall pattern when the block is repeated.

In pieced quilts, I am designing with the background as well as the foreground. The seams dividing the background of each of these blocks derive from the seams I draw to piece the vegetables. This integrates the background pieces in the construction process in a way that is quite different from appliqué.

Working within the limits of the piecing process forces a degree of abstraction. To make a block that captures the vegetable image and uses a limited number of pieces of fabric and types of seams is a challenge that I really enjoy.

As you look through these blocks, you will find that I often slightly mismatch the seams forming the edges of the vegetables. This is deliberate (I really can draw). The irregularity of the mismatched edges makes the images much more interesting and more alive than if I followed Quilt Tradition.

## Styles of Piecing

Three different styles of piecing are used in the book. Some blocks are sewn with straight seams only. Straight seams are technically the easiest to sew, especially if you use the freezer paper template method I will describe. Some of these straight-seam blocks are very simple, with only a few templates; some are much more complicated with many templates. Visually, the straight seams often produce more abstract designs of great dynamism.

Curved seams are more time-consuming and require careful clipping, matching, and pinning. Many curved-seam designs contain fewer pieces than the comparable straight-seam design, but each curve will be more time-consuming to sew. Curved seams are often graceful. The type of curve is somewhat limited by the practicalities of machine piecing.

Inset corner seams are used only in the pumpkin block. The straight edges of inset corner piecing maintain some of the dynamism of straight seams, but cut down on the number of pieces in the block. The sewing is trickier than sewing straight seams, but with practice I think you'll come to enjoy it.

## Degree of Difficulty

Straight-seam blocks are easier to sew than curved-seam blocks. Blocks with a few pieces are easier to sew than blocks with many pieces.

Big blocks (with big pieces) are easier to sew than little blocks.

To make any block easier to sew, make it bigger (even much bigger) than the minimum enlargement size suggested in the text.

The vegetable blocks are arranged in the book in alphabetical order, not by degree of difficulty.

## HOW TO USE THE BLOCKS

### The Block Diagram

Each block is illustrated with a small-scale Block Diagram. Each piece is labeled with a letter denoting the section and a number indicating the piecing order. Beneath each Block Diagram is an enlargement percentage suggesting the recommended minimum practical size to make the block pieceable.

You may, of course, enlarge the Block Diagram more than this suggested percentage. Bigger is always easier. Very large blocks often make dramatic wallhangings or bed quilts.

*In getting ready to sew a block, you will need to enlarge the Block Diagram (not the Piecing Diagram) on a copier to at least the minimum recommended size.*

### Making Enlargements

Many copiers can enlarge a maximum of 200%, some only 140%. If your copier cannot make the full enlargement in one step, enlarge the Block Diagram as much as you can for a first step. Then enlarge again as many times as necessary to reach the desired size.

You can figure enlargement percentages easily and precisely on a small calculator according to the following formula:

(Desired dimension) ÷ (Present dimension) x 100 = Enlargement Percentage

For example, if you want your block to be 14" high, and it is presently 5" high:

14 (inches) ÷ 5 (inches) = 2.8 x 100 = 280%

Enlarge the 5" block 280% to get the 14" desired size.

If the copier enlarges a maximum 200%, enlarge the 5" block at 200% to get a 10" block, then recalculate.

14 (inches) ÷ 10 (inches) = 1.4 x 100 = 140%

Enlarge the 10" block 140% to get your desired 14" block.

This sounds harder than it is. Just enter the numbers on a little calculator.

To calculate the enlargement percentage, the dimensions of the block must be in decimals. If your ruler is in $1/16$ths of an inch, use the following table to convert fractions of an inch to decimals:

| | | | |
|---|---|---|---|
| $1/16$ ▸ | .0625 | $9/16$ ▸ | .5625 |
| $1/8$ ▸ | .125 | $5/8$ ▸ | .625 |
| $3/16$ ▸ | .1875 | $11/16$ ▸ | .6875 |
| $1/4$ ▸ | .25 | $3/4$ ▸ | .75 |
| $5/16$ ▸ | .3125 | $13/16$ ▸ | .8125 |
| $3/8$ ▸ | .375 | $7/8$ ▸ | .875 |
| $7/16$ ▸ | .4375 | $15/16$ ▸ | .9375 |
| $1/2$ ▸ | .5 | | |

That is, $3^{7}/8$" would be entered on the calculator as 3.875. Round off numbers after you have done the calculation.

### The Piecing Diagram

Each Block Diagram has an accompanying Piecing Diagram. This is a picture of how the block is most easily sewn together in sections. Each piece is labeled with the same letter and number as the Block Diagram.

### The Sewing Directions

Next to the Piecing Diagram is a column of Sewing Directions, which describe the sewing order. The blocks were deliberately designed with the sewing process in mind. Follow these directions carefully to make the sewing easier. You may want to cross off each step as you finish it.

When developing blocks on your own, choose sewing order by following this rule of thumb:

Don't start sewing a seam unless you can sew the entire seam from start to finish. The exception to this is in puzzle seams. See Green Beans quilt, page 25.

### The Arrows

Each Piecing Diagram also contains small Arrows. These indicate in which direction to press the seam allowances to sculpt the surface of the quilt top, and bring the vegetable image forward.

The direction in which the seam allowance is pressed makes a considerable difference in what the finished block looks like.

Rather than pressing seam allowances towards the darker piece or the less bulky side, as is recommended in traditional quilting, I recommend pressing each seam to pad the edge of one piece. Pressing each seam under the vegetable and away from the background brings the vegetable image forward and flattens the background.

Quilting the background more densely than the vegetable image can further enhance this sculpturing.

## TEMPLATES

All of these blocks are designed to be sewn with templates. There are several methods of making templates. Which method to use depends on how many repeated blocks you intend to make.

It is well worth while learning to use templates in the old-fashioned way. Template piecing is much quicker for repeated blocks than foundation piecing, and with practice can be just as accurate. There are many designs easily pieced with templates which can't be done as foundation piecing, including all of the curved-seam blocks. In addition, template piecing lets you control the direction in which you press the seam allowances, which makes a tremendous difference in the look of the block.

## Making Templates for a Single Block
### Tracing on Freezer Paper

Trace the enlarged Block Diagram (not the Piecing Diagram) onto the shiny side of freezer paper using a fine-line permanent marker. (Sharpie® or Identi-pen™ are brands that work well.)

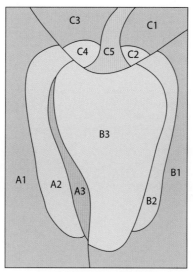

Bell Pepper block diagram

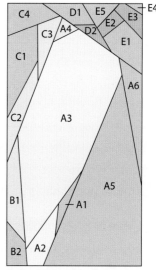

Italian Pepper block diagram

Enlarge the Block Diagram to the size at which you wish to sew.

## SHINY SIDE OF FREEZER PAPER

## DULL SIDE OF FREEZER PAPER

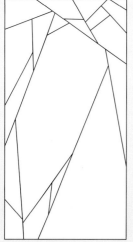

Trace enlarged block on shiny side of freezer paper.

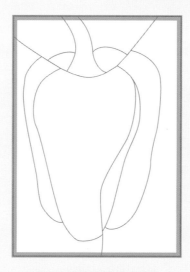

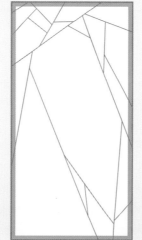

Highlight outside edge of block.

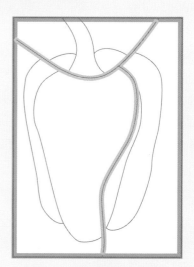

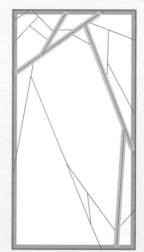

Highlight section lines.

## Labeling

Turn the freezer paper over, dull side up, and draw a line with a color highlighter or pencil (freehand is okay) just inside the outside edge of the block. After you have cut the freezer paper into separate pieces, this colored line will tell you what pieces form the outside edge of the block. For ease in sewing the blocks, put this colored edge on grain (lined up with the lengthwise or crosswise threads of the cloth) when ironing the freezer paper pieces to the back of the fabric.

Again, with the freezer paper dull side up, refer to the Piecing Diagram that accompanies each block and find the seams that divide the block into sections. Trace over these on the dull side of the freezer paper with a different color of highlighter or pencil. (Remember, the dull side of the freezer paper will be the reverse of the Piecing Diagram.)

## Tics

With a pencil draw short tic marks about every inch across the seams and mark small X's at the intersections, again on the dull side of the freezer paper. (Don't make tics closer

than 1" as it is then more likely that you may try to match the wrong tics).

With a pencil, label the pieces according to the Piecing Diagram. Looking at the dull side of the freezer paper, you will see the block reversed from the image in the Piecing Diagram. Label each section of your freezer paper, looking carefully at that section of the Piecing Diagram, rather than looking at the whole block. If the reversal is confusing, you may want to make a mirror-image copy of the Piecing Diagram.

| DULL SIDE OF FREEZER PAPER | | PIECING DIAGRAM |
|---|---|---|

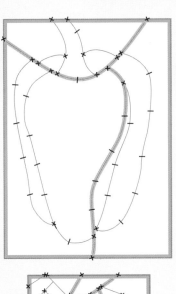

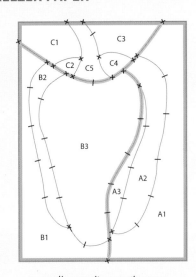

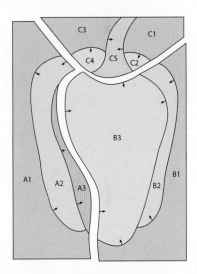

Mark tics along seams and X's at intersections.

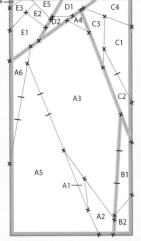

Label pieces according to the Piecing Diagram (reversed).

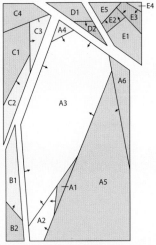

Label pieces according to the Piecing Diagram.

From the shiny side of the freezer paper, cut the freezer-paper block apart along the seam lines.

Iron each piece of freezer paper shiny side down on the back of your selected fabrics. Keep each piece of paper at least 1/2" from every other piece. Each piece of freezer paper is the finished size of the piece. We will be adding seam allowances. Adjust the temperature of the iron — if the iron is too cool the paper pieces will fall off.

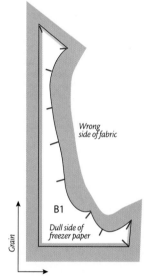

Cut freezer paper block apart and iron, shiny side down, on back of fabric. Put outside-edge pieces on grain.

## Changing Your Mind
One of the beauties of using freezer paper this way is that you can preview the cut block before you begin to sew. Lay or pin the fabric pieces (with the freezer paper on the back) on the original enlargement of the Block Diagram. The seam allowances will overlap, but you will be able to study your fabric choices. If a fabric displeases you, peel the freezer paper off, choose another fabric, iron on the paper piece, cut, and pin the new one in place.

You can reuse and re-iron each freezer-paper piece several times.

### Straight-Seam Blocks
## Adding Seam Allowances to Straight-Seam Blocks
On a cutting mat, using a clear ruler, align the 1/4" line of the ruler with the edge of the freezer paper. Cut with a rotary cutter along the edge of the ruler to add perfect 1/4" seam allowances. (Very slick!) Do not remove the freezer paper.

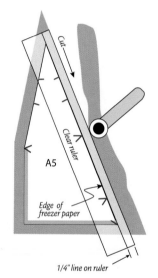

Place 1/4" line of ruler along edge of freezer paper. Cut with rotary cutter.

## Sewing Straight-Seam Blocks
Match edges and tic marks. Sew along the edge of the freezer paper. You can sew the whole block with the freezer paper on the back of the fabric pieces. The paper stabilizes the bias edges. Also very slick!

## Pressing
Press each seam, as you sew it, in the direction of the small arrows on the Piecing Diagram. I use a steam iron.

### Curved-Seam Blocks
## Adding Seam Allowances to Curved-Seam Blocks
Using a soft pencil, trace around each freezer-paper piece, drawing the seam line on the back of each fabric piece. I use soft colored art pencils in whatever color I can see best on the particular fabric.

Extend the tic marks into the seam allowance.

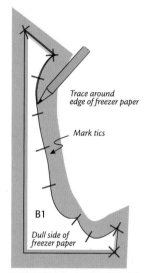

Mark seam line by tracing outside edge of freezer paper piece. Extend tic marks into seam allowance.

Cut out each fabric piece with scissors, leaving 1/4" seam allowance around the freezer paper. Cut the 1/4" as accurately as you can by eye. You will be matching and sewing along the penciled seam lines, so a precise 1/4" isn't absolutely critical. Do the best you can. Don't leave a seam allowance wider than 1/4" or the sewing will be harder than it needs to be. Don't leave a seam allowance smaller than 1/4", since then it is difficult to find your tic marks. There are rotary cutters that have an adjustable guide arm attachment to make it easy to add seam allowance and rotary cut simultaneously. I use scissors myself, but some students prefer to rotary cut.

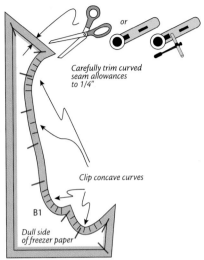

Carefully trim curved seam allowances to 1/4"

Clip concave curves

B1

Dull side of freezer paper

Carefully cut 1/4" seam allowance outside each freezer paper piece. Clip concave edges.

## Clipping Curves

Clip the seam allowances on the concave edges only. How many clips you should make and how close they come to the seam line will depend on the stretchiness of the fabric and the tightness of the curve. You can clip much more in a quilt top than you can in clothing construction because the backing/batting/ quilting will distribute the strain across the whole quilt, rather than on a single seam. You do not need to staystitch. Clipping the curves before removing the freezer paper will keep you from clipping too far.

## Sewing Curved-Seam Blocks

In order to manipulate the fabric as you sew curves, you will have to remove the freezer-paper pieces from the fabric pieces just before you sew. Pin each curve, matching seam lines and tic marks. Sew, using a slightly shorter stitch than usual, with the clips on top,

spreading them out to ease the process. Note that for an S-type curve, you will need to sew one section and then turn the unit over to sew the next section, always keeping the clips on top.

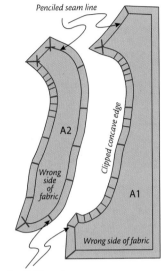

Penciled seam line

A2

Clipped concave edge

Wrong side of fabric

A1

Wrong side of fabric

Penciled tic marks

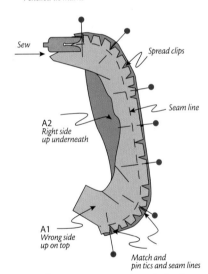

Sew

Spread clips

A2 Right side up underneath

Seam line

A1 Wrong side up on top

Match and pin tics and seam lines

Remove freezer paper, match and pin tics and seam lines. Sew with concave (clipped) piece on top, spreading clips.

I find it easier to sew curves with a 1/4" foot on the machine, rather than the wide zigzag one. You will need to be able to see clearly where the point of the needle enters the

fabric. For this reason, avoid 1/4" feet with a solid piece of metal in front of the needle. There should be a slot in front of the needle in the direction of the seam. I find 1/4" feet made from thick plastic or with a vertical metal fence at the edge awkward as well. With my Pfaff, I always piece using the even-feed feature, which I find really helps. You can also use a walking foot attachment if you have one for your brand of sewing machine. Some quilters change their throat plate to one with a single hole for straight piecing. (Just remember it's there and don't turn on the zigzag.)

## Pressing

Using a steam iron, press each seam allowance in the direction of the arrows on the Piecing Diagram. I do not trim extra fabric from the seam allowances, but consider it as extra padding.

Tape the used freezer paper pieces back together to keep track of them after you have removed them from the fabric.

### Inset Corner Blocks
### Adding Seam Allowances to Inset Corner Blocks

On a cutting mat, using a clear ruler, align the 1/4" line of the ruler with the edge of the freezer paper. As with regular straight-seam blocks, cut with a rotary cutter along the edge of the ruler to add perfect 1/4" seam allowances. Be careful on inner corners not to cut too far.

## Marking and Clipping Inset Corners

Mark dots on the wrong side of the fabric at each corner or bend. Clip to the dot at inner corners. I usually remove the freezer paper at this point. Some students have told me they prefer to leave it on, and sew along its edge.

## Sewing Inset Corners

You will be sewing with the clipped piece on top. Pin and match the first two dots. Shorten the stitch length to 1.5 (or 15 on an older American machine). Set the machine "needle down" if possible. Start on the edge; stitch to the first dot, removing the pin. Leaving the needle down in the dot, raise the presser foot. Pivot the lower piece on the needle to line up the next seam. Very gently, swing the top piece on the needle. Match the next dots on both pieces. Lower the presser foot and continue sewing.

## Pressing

Press with a steam iron in the direction of the arrows. I do not trim excess fabric at the bends in the seam allowances, but consider it extra padding.

## Making Templates for a Few Repeated Blocks

You can make up to four copies of your freezer paper block at one time (shiny or dull side up, depending on whether you want any blocks to be reversed). Stack four pieces of freezer paper. Put your traced block on top. Staple or pin the layers together.

Remove the top thread from your sewing machine. With an old needle and a short stitch length, sew through all layers following the lines on your traced block. This will perforate each layer of paper with your block pattern.

Use each freezer paper copy as described for single blocks.

## Making Templates for Many Repeated Blocks

One of the easiest ways to make plastic templates is to start with a paper copy of your block at the size you want to sew. Label the pieces in the block according to the Block Diagram. Mark tics at intersections and about 1" apart along seam lines. (Don't make tics closer than 1", as it is then more likely that you may try to match the wrong tics). Cut the paper block apart. Glue or tape each paper piece to template plastic. Cut out each plastic template leaving ¼" seam allowance outside the paper. With a ⅛" hole punch (available at craft stores) punch a small hole at each tic and corner.

Fabrics can be stack-cut with these plastic templates. Layer four to eight fabrics wrong side up. Iron the stack with a steam iron. Put the plastic template on top, wrong side up. Either trace the template with a pencil, then cut the stack with very sharp scissors, or cut using a ruler and rotary cutter.

For more accurate sewing, mark a small pencil dot through the punched holes on the back of each fabric piece. Match and pin the dots together as needed before sewing each seam.

## FABRIC SELECTION

It's great fun to try to find fabrics that mimic the colors and textures of the different vegetables. Try to find a subtle stripe for celery, a stippled texture for the broccoli heads, or a shaded fabric from which to cut the artichoke leaves. You may be able to use the right side of a fabric for the outer darker lettuce leaves, and the paler wrong side for the inner leaves.

Some fabrics can be fussy-cut (that is, a very particular part of a print selectively cut) to make the shiny spot on an eggplant or tomato.

I love to mix fabrics for backgrounds. It makes the block design much richer and more exciting than simply cutting all of the background pieces from one fabric. This is especially true when repeating a single block, as you can see in the small quilt designs included with each block.

In the sampler quilt of all of the blocks, I used a variety of blue fabrics for curved-seam blocks and a variety of dark browns for straight-seam blocks.

Using printed fabrics with bright light or white bits in the print adds a sparkle to the surface of the quilt – little gleams of sunlight or dew drops. You will see many of them in the background and sashing fabrics in the sampler quilt.

the
Vegetable
blocks

Artichoke

# Artichoke
## *Curved Seams*

For this block, I fussy-cut a printed fabric to have a purple tint on tips of the artichoke leaves. On the dull side of freezer paper or plastic templates, mark the tip of each leaf as an aid in placing the templates on the shaded fabric correctly.

Because of the curved seams and number of pieces, this block is one of the more difficult ones to sew. Making it bigger than the minimum recommended size will make it easier.

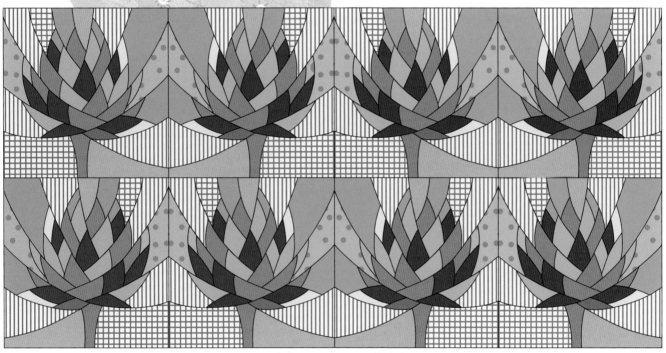

Artichoke curved-seam quilt design

In this quilt design, I've reversed every other block to create the interesting secondary design where the seams meet.

The size suggested is the minimum practical sewing size. To make it easier, make it bigger. During construction press the seam allowance in the direction indicated by the arrows on the piecing diagram.

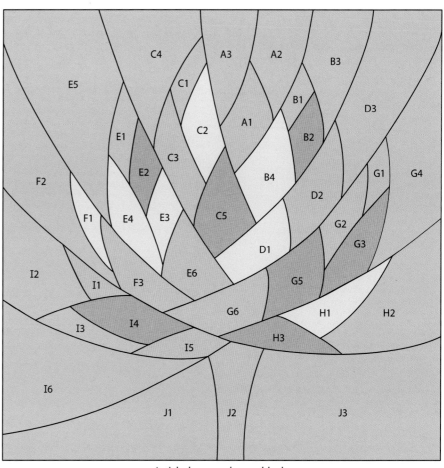

Artichoke curved-seam block
Enlarge this block 213% to a 10" x 10" square, see page 9.

Sew:
A1 to A2 to A3
B1 to B2 to B3 to B4 to A
C1 to C2 to C3 to C4 to C5 to AB
D1 to D2 to D3 to ABC
E1 to E2 to E3 to E4 to E5 to E6 to ABCD
F1 to F2 to F3 to ABCDE
G1 to G2 to G3 to G4 to G5 to G6 to ABCDEF
H1 to H2 to H3 to ABCGEFG
I1 to I2, I3 to I4 to I(1,2) to I5 to I6
J1 to J2 to J3 to I to ABCDEFGH

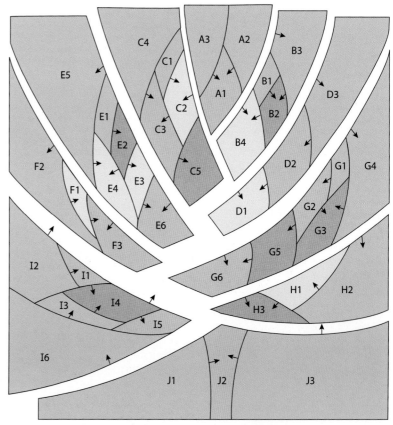

Artichoke curved-seam piecing diagram

# Asparagus

Spring is here when
the first asparagus shoots
poke up through the soil.

# Asparagus
## *Straight Seams*

Although I have pieced asparagus at 15" x 5", it could easily be two or three times that size. Mark the small templates in sections A and C carefully. You may want to use a different color pencil for each tic in sections A and C since many of the pieces are a similar size and shape. When doing this kind of complicated piecing, I often sew the smallest pieces first.

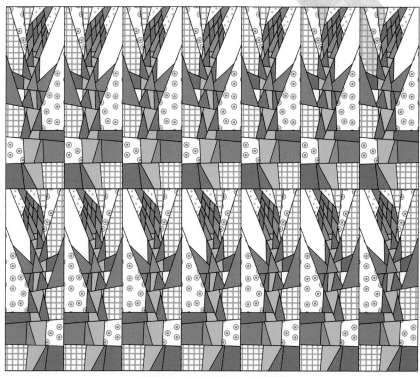

The blocks in the bottom row are the reverse of the blocks in the top row.

Asparagus straight-seam quilt design

Two asparagus blocks, four reverse blocks. Cut rectangles to fill in above and below each block to make a rectangular quilt.

Asparagus straight-seam quilt design

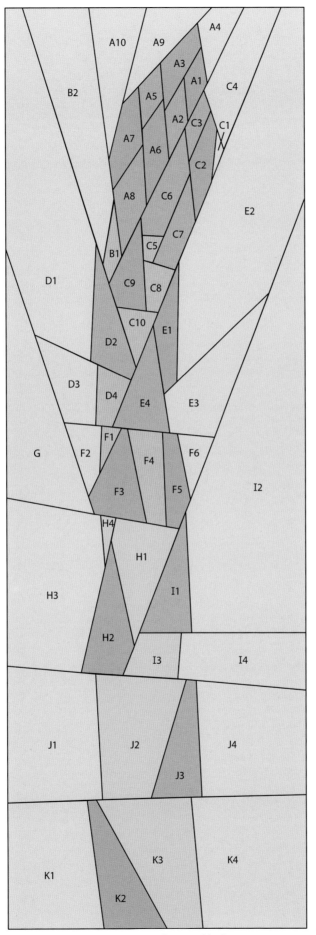

Asparagus straight-seam block
Enlarge this block 155% to a 15" x 5" rectangle, see page 9.

The size suggested is the minimum practical sewing size. To make it easier, make it bigger. During construction press the seam allowance in the direction indicated by the arrows on the piecing diagram.

Sew:

A1 to A2 to A3 to A4

A5 to A6 to A(1,2,3,4)

A7 to A8 to A(1,2,3,4,5,6) to A9 to A10

B1 to B2 to A

C1 to C2 to C3 to C4

C5 to C6 to C7 to C(1,2,3,4) to C8 to C9 to
C10 to AB

D1 to D2, D3 to D4 to D(1,2) to ABC

E1 to E2 to E3 to E4 to ABCD

F1 to F2 to F3 to F4 to F5 to F6 to ABCDE to G

H1 to H2, H3 to H4 to H(1,2) to ABCDEFG

I1 to I2, I3 to I4 to I(1,2) to ABCDEFGH

J1 to J2 to J3 to J4 to ABCDEFGHI

K1 to K2 to K3 to K4 to ABCDEFGHIJ

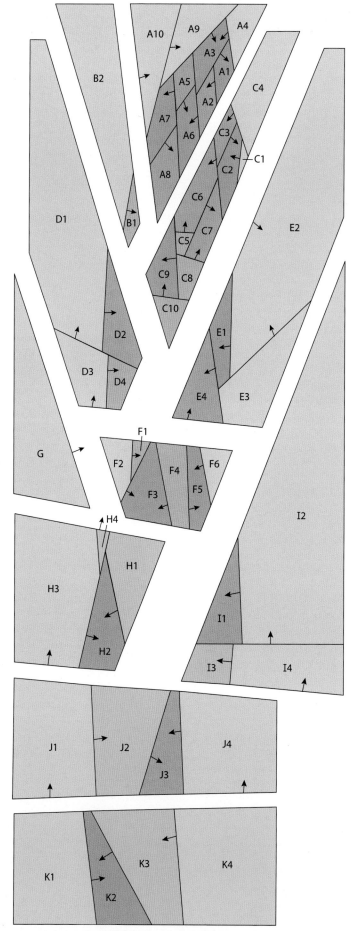

Asparagus straight-seam piecing diagram

# Green Beans

Green pods, purple pods, or
the lovely pale yellow of wax
beans are all possibilities here.

# Green Beans
## *Straight Seams*

I've set up this quilt design as a pinwheel pattern of the rectangular bean blocks. The pattern requires the addition of small squares to fill out the surface. The dimension of the small squares is the difference between the length and width of the bean block. For a 13" x 8" bean block, the square is 5" x 5".

The squares are puzzle pieces. To sew rectangle blocks together with the squares, start by sewing a square and the long side of a rectangle with a partial seam.

Green beans straight-seam quilt design

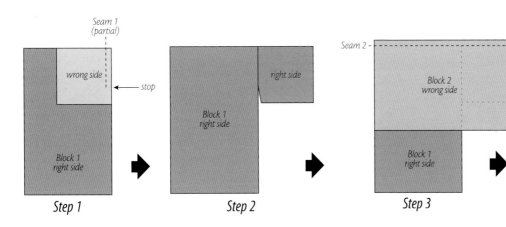

## PARTIAL SEAM ASSEMBLY

The sewing of the puzzle piece (the square in this case) is most easily done this way. Begin by joining the square to the first block with a partial seam.

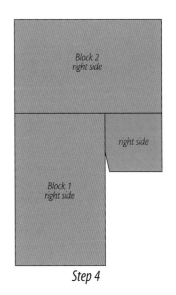

*Step 1*

*Step 2*

*Step 3*

*Step 4*

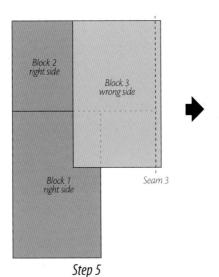

*Step 5*

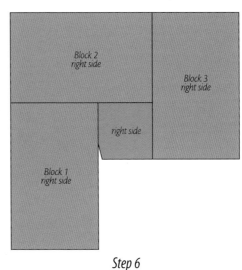

*Step 6*

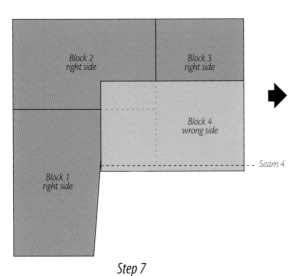

*Step 7*

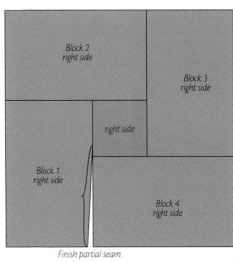

*Step 8*

The size suggested is the minimum practical sewing size. To make it easier, make it bigger. During construction press the seam allowance in the direction indicated by the arrows on the piecing diagram.

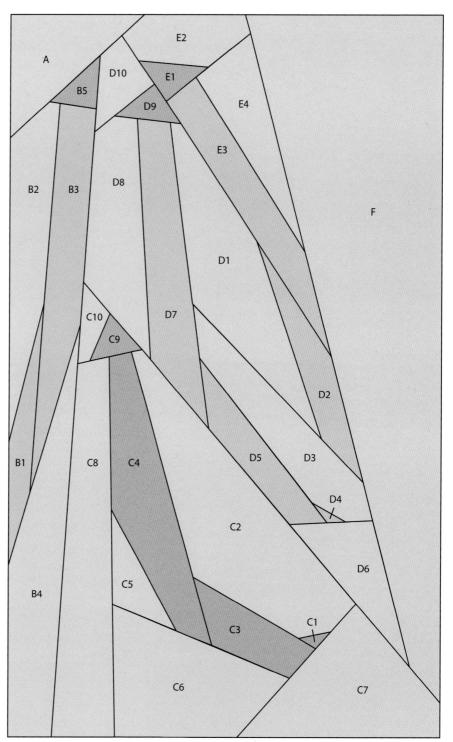

Green beans straight-seam block
Enlarge this block 172% to a 13" x 8" rectangle, see page 9.

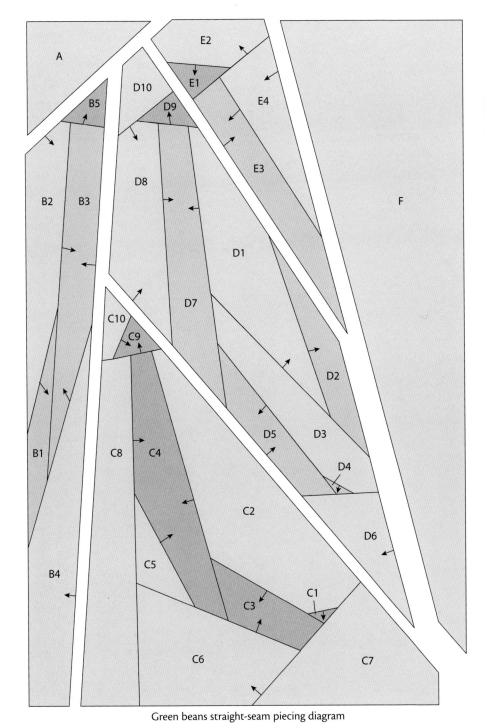

Sew:
B1 to B2 to B3 to B4 to B5
C1 to C2 to C3 to C4 to C5 to C6 to C7 to C8
C9 to C10 to C(1,2,3,4,5,6,7,8)
D1 to D2 to D3 to D4 to D5 to D6 to D7 to D8
to D9 to D10
E1 to E2, E3 to E4 to E(1,2) to D to F to C
to B to A

Green beans straight-seam piecing diagram

# Shell Beans

The seeds of shell beans come in wonderful colors, sometimes with colored pods as well. One old variety is called Tongues of Fire.

# Shell Beans
## *Curved Seams*

Here are two variations for quilt designs. The first design (lower left) uses two blocks and two reverse blocks. The second design (below) uses blocks that rotate around a central square. The dimension of the square is the difference between the length and width of the block.

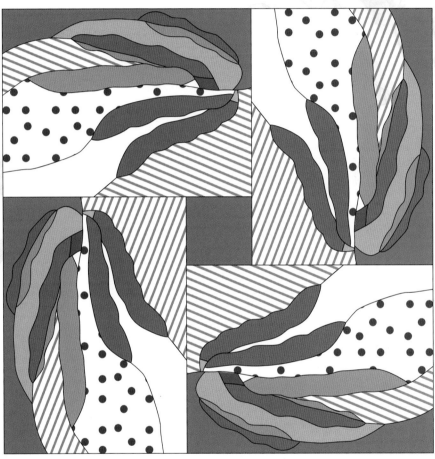

Shell beans curved-seam quilt designs

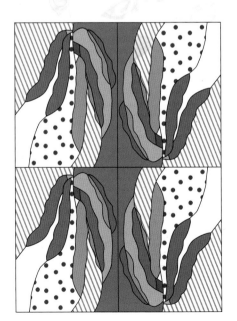

The size suggested is the minimum practical sewing size. To make it easier, make it bigger. During construction press the seam allowance in the direction indicated by the arrows on the piecing diagram.

This block is one of the trickiest in this book to sew because of the undulating seams on the sides of the pods. I clipped all the concave curves, pinned carefully and sewed each undulating seam in one pass, carefully manipulating the fabrics with my fingertips to match the edges and seam lines. In sewing an undulating seam like this, half of the clips will be in the top fabric and half of the clips in the bottom fabric.

Consider enlarging this block to twice the 15" x 11" size. Sewing the undulating seam would be a little easier and it would make a stunning quilt.

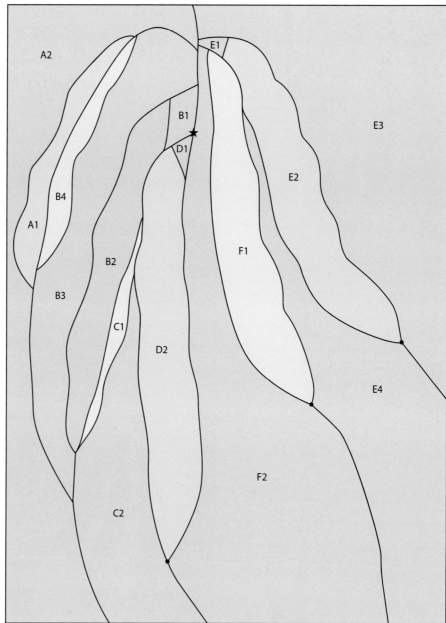

Shell beans curved-seam block
Enlarge this block 232% to a 15" x 11" rectangle, see page 9.

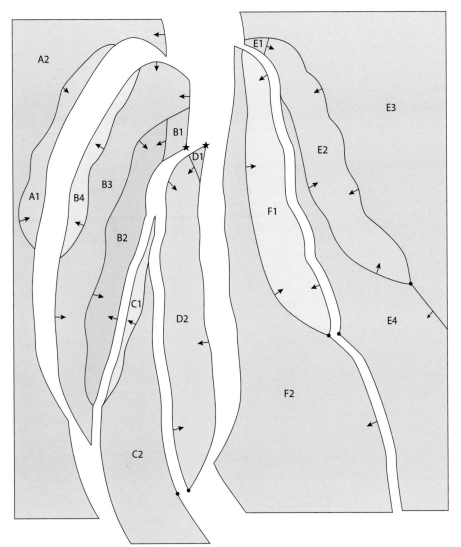

Sew:
A1 to A2
B1 to B2 to B3 to B4 to A
C1 to C2 to AB
D1 to D2 to ABC from ★ to •
E1 to E2 to E3 (backstitch at •)
E2 to E4 (backstitch at •)
E3 to E4 (backstitch at •)
F1 to F2 (backstitch at •)
F2 to E4 (backstitch at •)
finish FE seam
ABD to EF (backstitch at •)
finish CF seam

Shell beans curved-seam piecing diagram
All •'s are Y seams. Backstitch each seam at the •'s.

# Beets

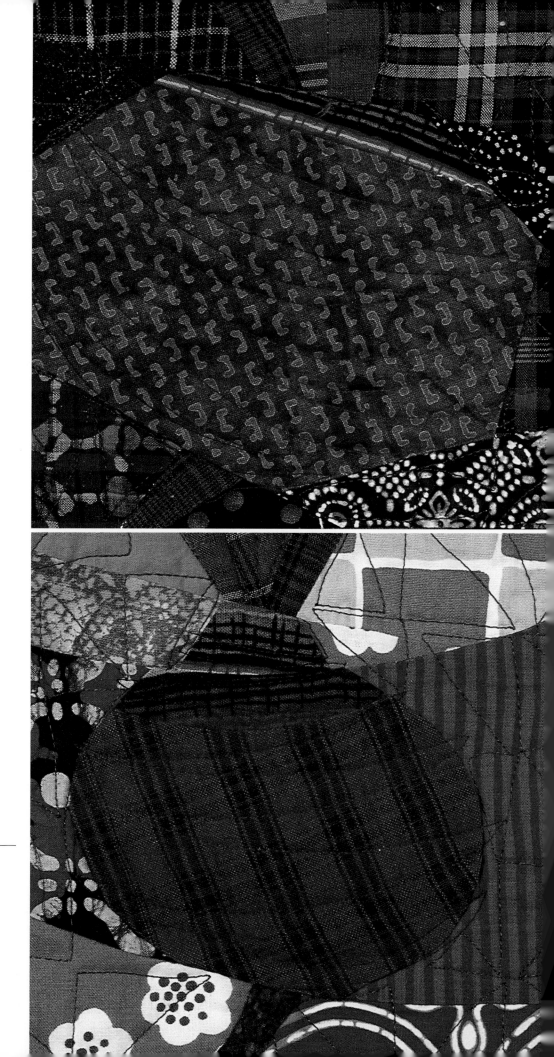

From inside this humble root crop comes the most glorious red juice. Alas, the color is fugitive when you try to use it as a fabric dye.

# Beets
## *Straight Seams*

The red or gold colors of beets glow against a dark earthy background. Beet stems frequently have both red and green parts. Perhaps you can find a small red/green stripe for the stem pieces A2, A3, and A4.

Each straight-seam quilt design is made of six identical blocks. In the first, all the blocks are oriented with the tops up. In the second design, they are positioned in four different directions.

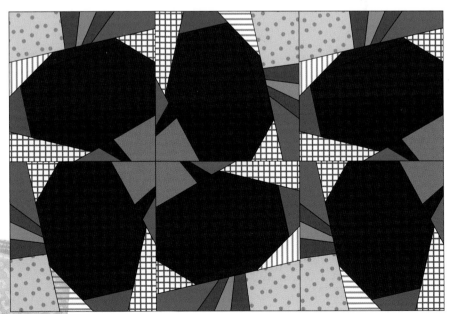

Beet straight-seam quilt designs

The size suggested is the minimum practical sewing size. To make it easier, make it bigger. During construction press the seam allowance in the direction indicated by the arrows on the piecing diagram.

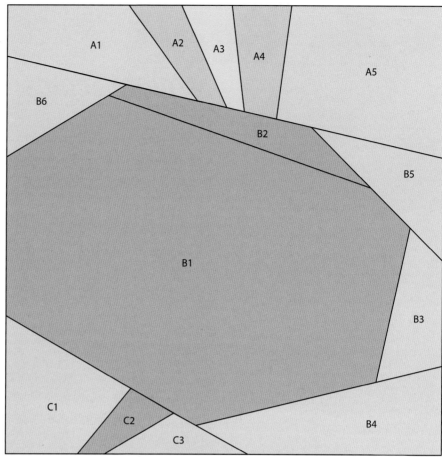

Beet straight-seam block
Enlarge this block 128% to a 6" x 6" square, see page 9.

Sew:
A1 to A2 to A3 to A4 to A5
B1 to B2 to B3 to B4 to B5 to B6 to A
C1 to C2 to C3 to AB

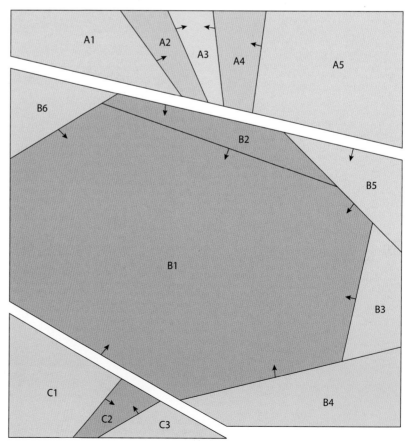

Beet straight-seam piecing diagram

# Beets
## Curved Seams

The roundness of the beets enhances the rhythm of these two quilt designs. The first has a row of upside-down beets on the bottom so the roots meet in the center, forming a secondary pattern. The second design uses two sets of four beets in a pinwheel pattern.

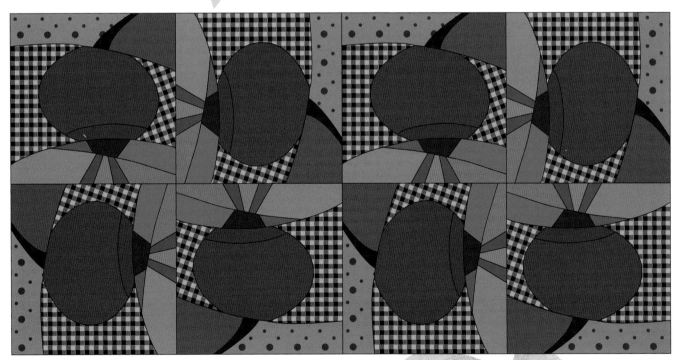

Beet curved-seam quilt designs

While I don't usually trim seam allowances, the root (D2) of this curved-seam beet will be easier to sew if you do. After sewing D1 to D2, trim the seam allowances slightly so they don't interfere with adding D3. Press seams in the directions of the arrows. This will place all the seam allowances under the beet root.

The size suggested is the minimum practical sewing size. To make it easier, make it bigger. During construction press the seam allowance in the direction indicated by the arrows on the piecing diagram.

Sew:
A1 to A2 to A3 to A4 to A5 (can be flip and sew)
B1 to B2 to B3 to A
C1 to C2 to C3 to C4 to AB
D1 to D2 to D3 to ABC

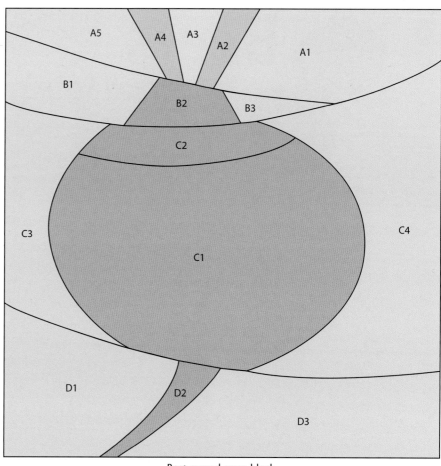

Beet curved-seam block
Enlarge this block 128% to a 6" x 6" square, see page 9.

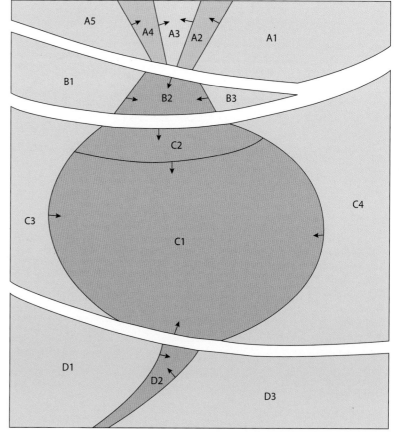

Beet curved-seam piecing diagram

Broccoli

# Broccoli
## Straight and Curved Seams

In addition to containing both straight and curved seams, this block is constructed with Y seams at a number of intersections. I try to avoid designing these Y seams, as they are tedious in machine piecing, but it was the best way I could find to make this block look like broccoli. Sewing this block is like sewing a Grandmother's Flower Garden quilt.

The fabric in the broccoli head was fussy-cut from a mottled print, keeping the lighter sections at the top of the florets. If you choose to do that too, write on the dull side of the freezer paper where you want the lights and darks to be. This will make it much easier to place the pieces on the fabric correctly.

This quilt design uses eight blocks and eight reverse blocks, forming an interesting symmetry pattern.

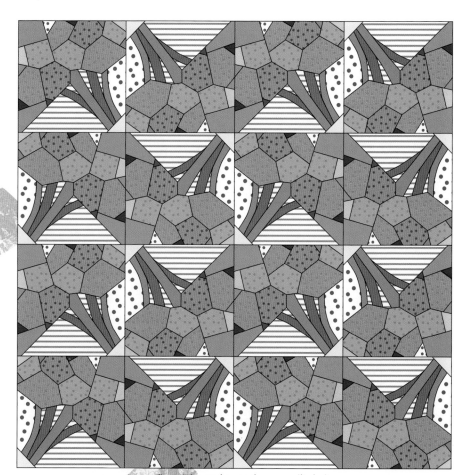

Broccoli straight- and curved-seam quilt design

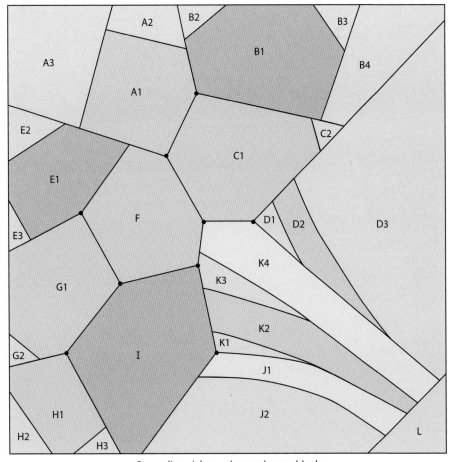

Broccoli straight- and curved-seam block
Enlarge this block 192% to a 9" x 9" square, see page 9.

The size suggested is the minimum practical sewing size. To make it easier, make it bigger. During construction press the seam allowance in the direction indicated by the arrows on the piecing diagram.

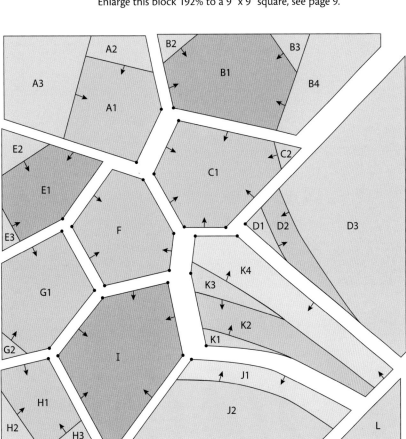

Broccoli straight- and curved-seam piecing diagram. All •'s are Y seams.
Backstitch each seam at the •, instead of sewing from the cut edge of the fabric piece.

Sew:
A1 to A2 to A3
B1 to B2 to B3 to B4 to A
C1 to C2 to B to A
D1 to D2 to D3 to ABC
E1 to E2 to E3 to F to ABCD
G1 to G2 to E to F
H1 to H2 to H3 to G
H to I, G to I, I to F
K1 to K2 to K3 to K4 to C, K to F, K to I, K to D
J1 to J2 to I, J to K, JKD to L

Cabbage

# Cabbage
## Straight Seams

In the first quilt design, the cabbage block is rotated back and forth. In the second quilt design, the cabbage blocks form a pinwheel.

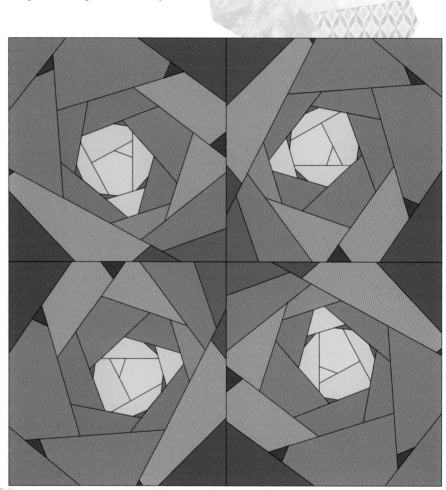

Cabbage straight-seam quilt designs

This cabbage block is a modified log-cabin in terms of construction. If desired, section A in the piecing diagram could be paper pieced on the freezer-paper pattern, rather than cutting the paper pieces of section A apart and template piecing them.

The little pieces A6, A7, A8, and A9 should be cut from dark fabrics as shadows to separate the tight center of the cabbage from the loose outer leaves. If template piecing section A, press the seams joining A6, A7, A8, and A9 toward the center to round and lift the center ball of the cabbage. If paper (foundation) piecing section A, these seams will naturally fall away from the center.

The size suggested is the minimum practical sewing size. To make it easier, make it bigger. During construction press the seam allowance in the direction indicated by the arrows on the piecing diagram.

Sew:
A1 to A2 to A3 to A4 toA5 to A6 to A7 to A8 to A9 to A10 to A11 to A12 to A13 to A14 to A15 to A16 to A17 to A18 to A19
B1 to B2 to A
C1 to C2 to AB
D1 to D2 to ABC
E1 to E2 to E3 to E4 to ABCD to F to G

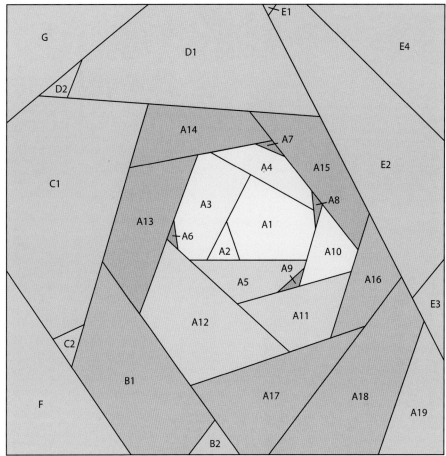

Cabbage straight-seam block
Enlarge this block 213% to a 10" x 10" square.

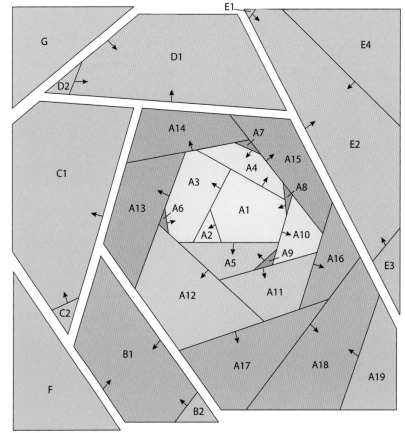

Cabbage straight-seam piecing diagram

Carrots

# Carrots
## *Straight Seams*

Did you know that carrots were once yellow or black? Almost all of the garden varieties presently in use are orange. Maybe some seed company will develop a rainbow of carrot colors for our delight.

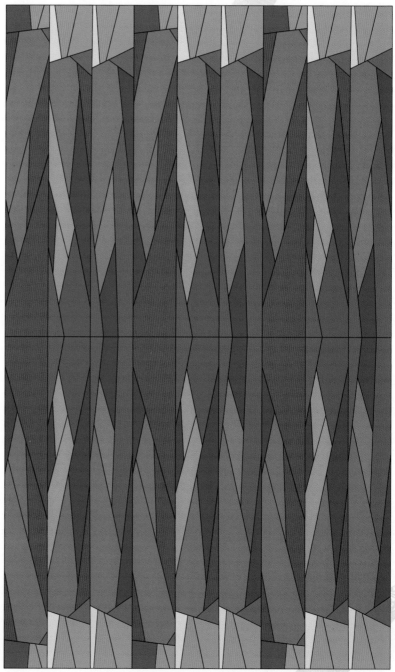

This quilt uses three blocks and three reverse blocks, creating a mirror image.

Carrot straight-seam quilt design

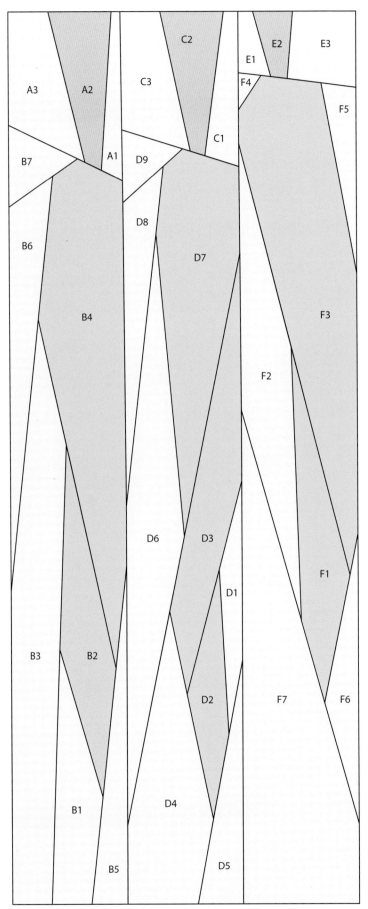

Carrot straight-seam block
Enlarge this block 161% to a 15" x 6" rectangle, see page 9.

The three carrots in this block are each in a 15" x 2" rectangle, three little blocks within the bigger 15" x 6" one. Rearrange the little blocks within the larger block if you want to give more variety to a quilt of many blocks.

The size suggested is the minimum practical sewing size. To make it easier, make it bigger. During construction press the seam allowance in the direction indicated by the arrows on the piecing diagram.

Sew:
A1 to A2 to A3
B1 to B2 to B3 to B4 to B5 to B6 to B7 to A
C1 to C2 to C3
D1 to D2 to D3 to D4 to D5
D6 to D7 to D8 to D9 to D(1,2,3,4,5) to C to AB
E1 to E2 to E3
F1 to F2 to F3 to F4 to F5 to F6 to F7 to
E to ABCD

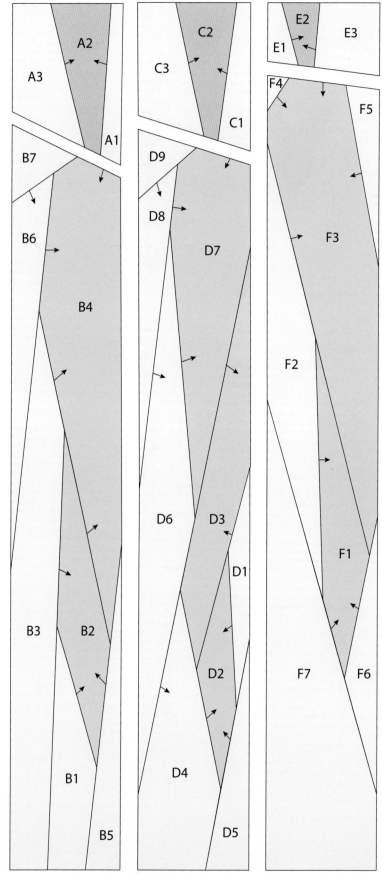

Carrot straight-seam piecing diagram

# Carrots
## *Curved Seams*

A single carrot this time — piecing within the carrot itself lets you use six different fabrics to shade the carrot from top to root end. If you'd rather simplify the piecing, cut (B1, B2, B3, B4, B5, and B6) from a single fabric, solid, striped, or shaded.

In the small quilt design I've drawn four carrot blocks and four reversed blocks, shifting the columns of carrots down like stair steps. You can fill in at the top and bottom of each column with rectangles to make a rectangular quilt.

Carrot curved-seam quilt design

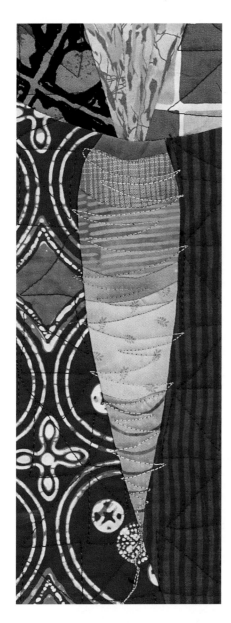

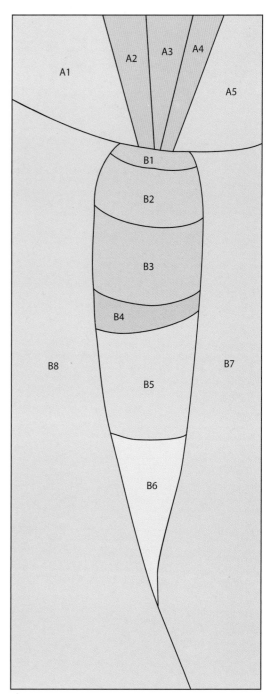

Carrot curved-seam block
Enlarge this block 149%
to a 10½" x 4" rectangle, see page 9.

The size suggested is the minimum practical sewing size. To make it easier, make it bigger. During construction press the seam allowance in the direction indicated by the arrows on the piecing diagram.

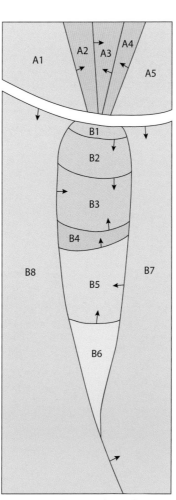

Carrot curved-seam piecing diagram

Sew:
A1 to A2 to A3 to A4 to A5
B1 to B2 to B3 to B4 to B5 to B6 to B7
to B8 to A

# celery

Cool and crunchy with
fragrant leaves, celery is
indispensable in many
recipes as well as a
treat by itself.

# Celery
## Straight Seams

Here's a good place to use some fabrics with narrow stripes of green. It's great fun to search your stash or the fabric store for perfect celery or carrot fabrics.

Be very careful with the top edge of this block after you have sewn it. Because of the number of seams along the top edge, it is very easy to stretch this edge wider than you had planned. It will be a real test if you can make this block this small. You'll be much happier with a block at least 13" x 6½", or even bigger.

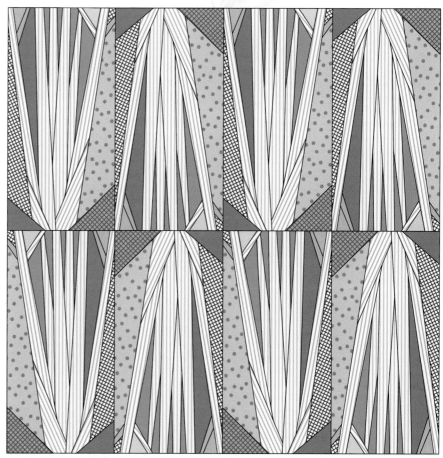

Celery straight-seam quilt design

For this quilt design, I used four blocks and four reverse blocks, and alternated the orientation in each row. There's a short poem about celery by Ogden Nash that would be fun to quilt in a border.

The size suggested is the minimum practical sewing size. To make it easier, make it bigger. During construction press the seam allowance in the direction indicated by the arrows on the piecing diagram.

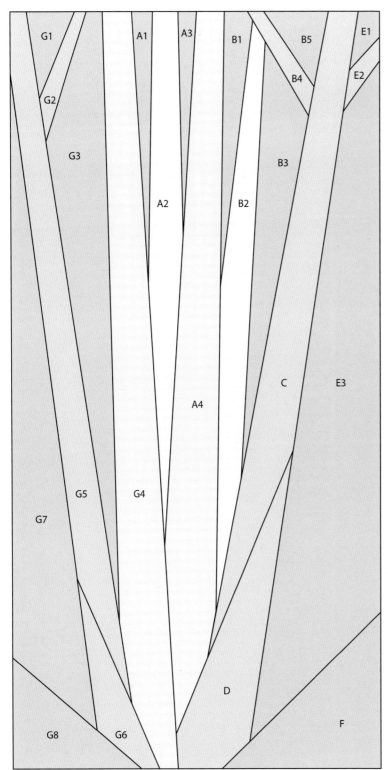

Celery straight-seam block
Enlarge this block 126% to a 10" x 5" rectangle, see page 9.

Sew: A1 to A2 to A3 to A4
B1 to B2 to B3 to B4 to B5 to A to C to D
E1 to E2 to E3 to ABCD to F
G1 to G2 to G3 to G4 to G5 to G6 to G7 to G8
to ABCDEF

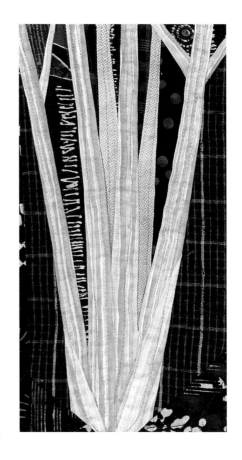

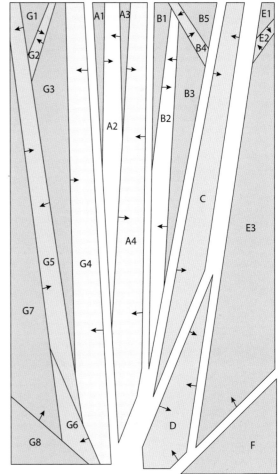

Celery straight-seam piecing diagram

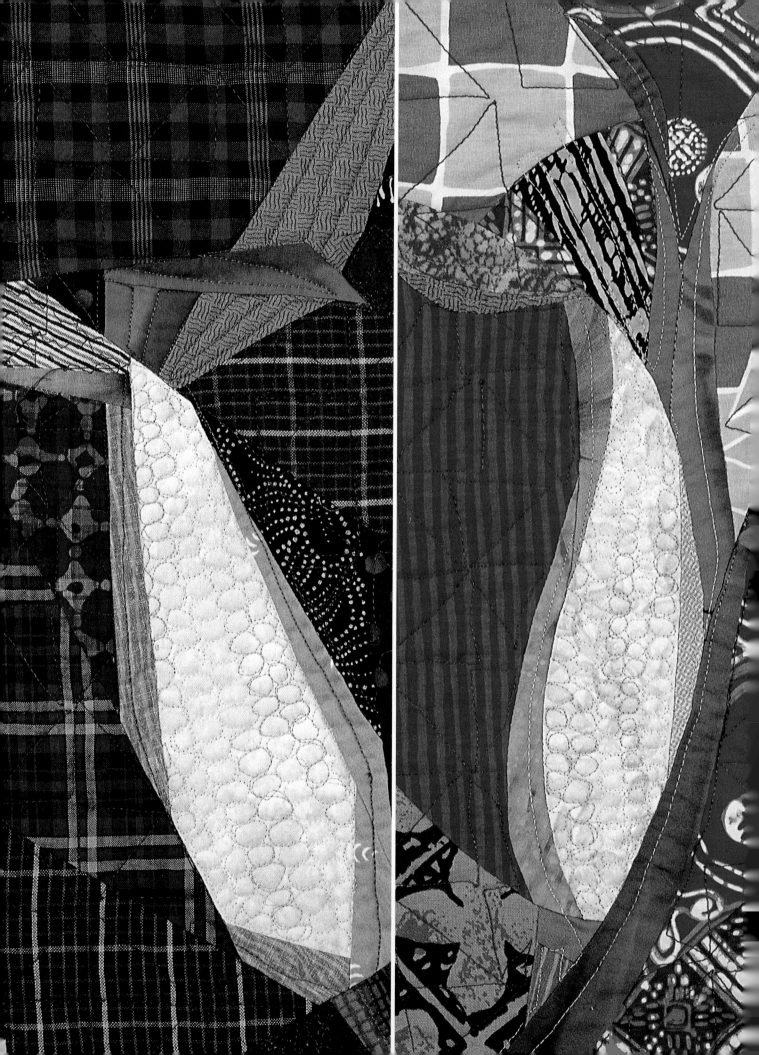

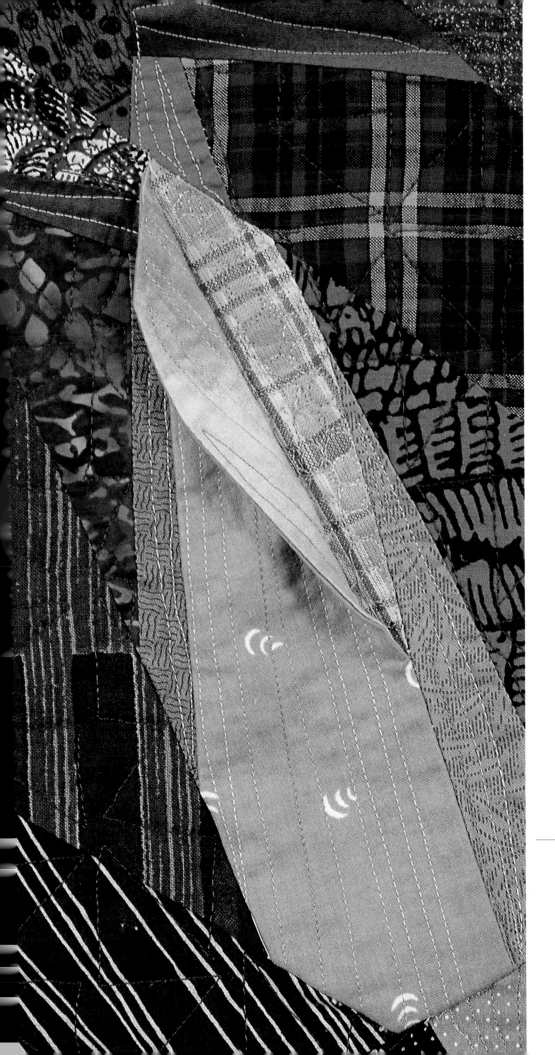

# Corn

As asparagus is the sign of spring, the first sweet corn means summer has arrived. Have the water heating when you go out to pick the ears.

# Corn
## Straight Seams

Corn is an American plant, native to the New World, as are potatoes, tomatoes, and peppers. In addition to the yellow and white kernels most familiar as sweet corn, corn kernels may be blue, red, burgundy, purple, orange, or striped.

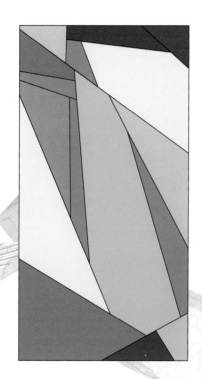

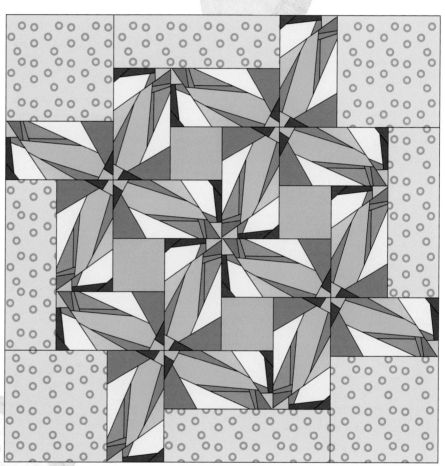

Corn 1 straight-seam quilt design

This quilt design is a pinwheel of blocks with the addition of background squares and rectangles to fill out the top. The dimension of the squares is the difference between the length and width of the block, in this case, a 5" x 5" square. This square is a "puzzle piece" which requires partial seams in the sewing process. See Green Beans, page 25, for sewing directions.

The twists and turns of the leaf blades are much more elaborate in this straight seam corn block, and the block itself somewhat larger. I especially like the diagonal leaf moving to the upper right in opposition to the diagonal of the corn ear.

For the quilt design, I have made half of the blocks reversed and staggered the horizontal rows so that a reverse block is over a plain block and a plain block over a reverse.

Corn 2 straight-seam quilt design

I've designed a simple straight-seam block that has a number of options. It can be a simple pieced block as shown. Pieces A1, A3, B1, B3, B5, B6 and C2 can be cut from a variety of greens to make an ear of corn with the husks intact. Or piece B5 can be cut from yellow, white, or yellow-and-white to make a partially husked ear of sweet corn. Or piece B5, the kernels, can be cut from red, yellow, blue, white, or multi-colored plaid to make a decorative dried ear. In that case, A1, A3, B1, B3, B6, and C2 should be the light straw color of dried husks. Piece B4 in each case represents the corn silk, pale yellow green in a young ear or dark brown in a mature ear.

To vary the block, you can make a faced flap for a husk that folds back from piece B5, as shown on the next page.

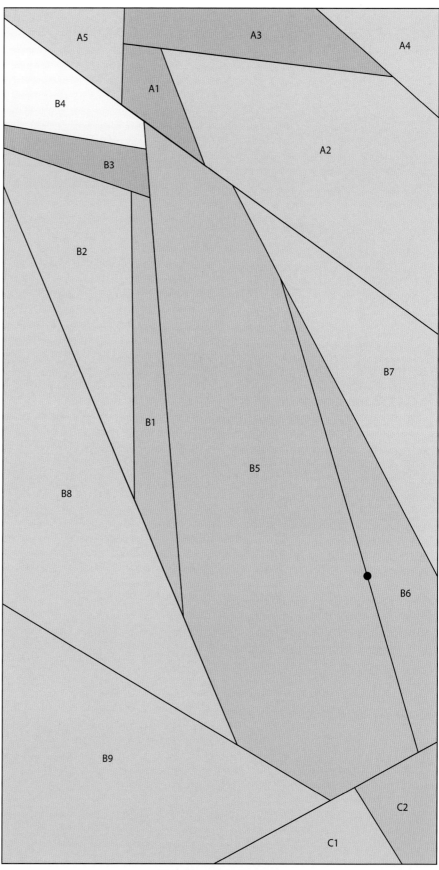

Corn 1 straight-seam block
Enlarge this block 117% to a 10½" x 5½" rectangle, see page 9.

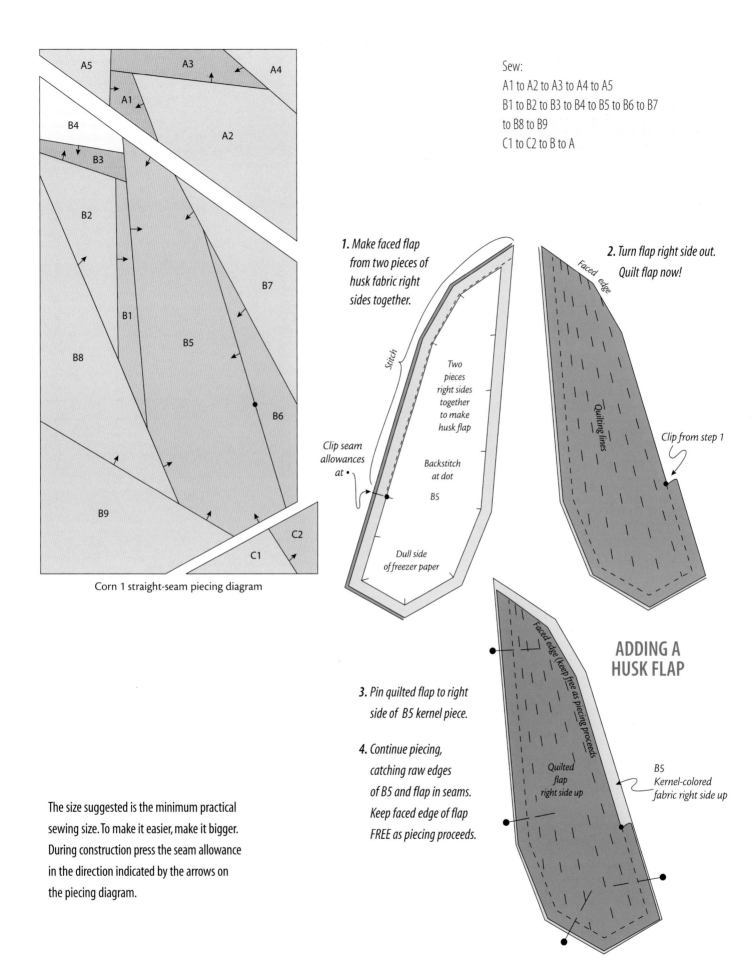

A5 A3 A4 A1 B4 A2 B3 B2 B1 B7 B5 B8 B6 B9 C2 C1

Corn 1 straight-seam piecing diagram

Sew:
A1 to A2 to A3 to A4 to A5
B1 to B2 to B3 to B4 to B5 to B6 to B7
to B8 to B9
C1 to C2 to B to A

**1.** Make faced flap from two pieces of husk fabric right sides together.

Stitch

Two pieces right sides together to make husk flap

Backstitch at dot

B5

Clip seam allowances at •

Dull side of freezer paper

**2.** Turn flap right side out. Quilt flap now!

Faced edge

Quilting lines

Clip from step 1

## ADDING A HUSK FLAP

**3.** Pin quilted flap to right side of B5 kernel piece.

**4.** Continue piecing, catching raw edges of B5 and flap in seams. Keep faced edge of flap FREE as piecing proceeds.

Faced edge (keep free as piecing proceeds)

Quilted flap right side up

B5 Kernel-colored fabric right side up

The size suggested is the minimum practical sewing size. To make it easier, make it bigger. During construction press the seam allowance in the direction indicated by the arrows on the piecing diagram.

This block could also be colored several ways, with piece C2 being either the husk or the kernels.

The size suggested is the minimum practical sewing size. To make it easier, make it bigger. During construction press the seam allowance in the direction indicated by the arrows on the piecing diagram.

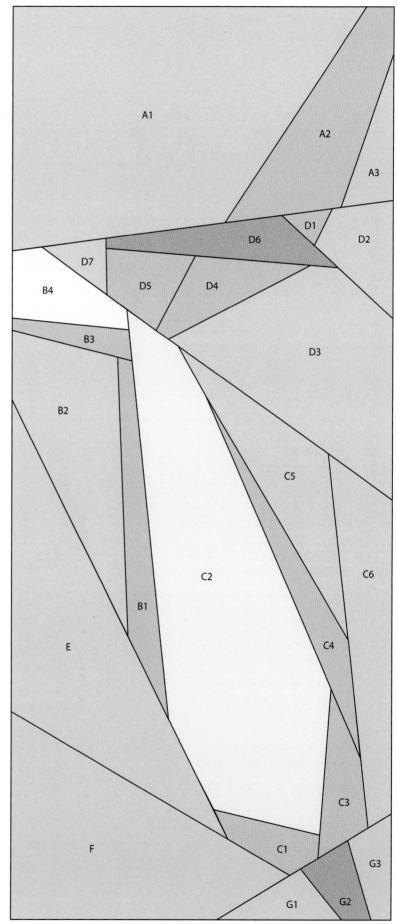

Corn 2 straight-seam block
Enlarge this block 147% to a 14" x 6" rectangle, see page 9.

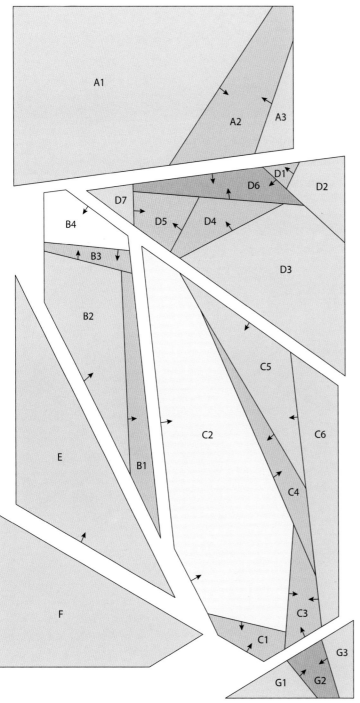

Sew:
A1 to A2 to A3
B1 to B2 to B3 to B4
C1 to C2 to C3 to C4 to C5 to C6 to B
D1 to D2
D3 to D4 to D5 to D6 to D7 to D(1,2) to BC to A
G1 to G2 to G3
ABCD to E to F to G

Corn 2 straight-seam piecing diagram

# Corn
## Curved Seams

Very gentle curves produce an elegant design, reminiscent of the Art Nouveau style. Enlarged even further than the suggested minimum size, to a 19½" x 7½" (203%) rectangle, this could be a very nice wallhanging.

I have suggested two different quilt designs. The first one is similar to Corn 2 quilt design. The second is a very unusual set and will require some partial seams when joining the blocks together.

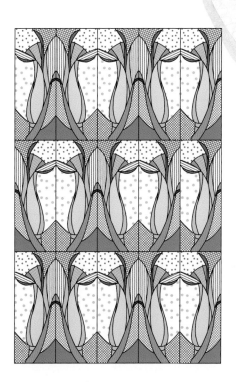

Corn curved-seam quilt designs

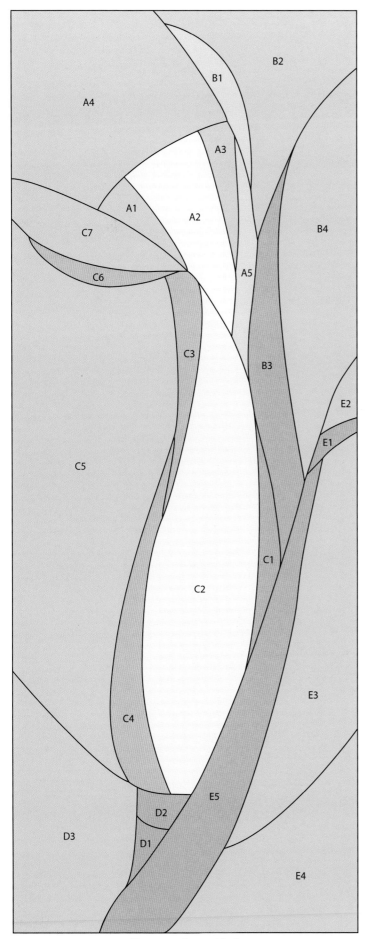

The size suggested is the minimum practical sewing size. To make it easier, make it bigger. During construction press the seam allowance in the direction indicated by the arrows on the piecing diagram.

Corn curved-seam block
Enlarge this block 135% to a 13" x 5" rectangle, see page 9.

Sew:
A1 to A2 to A3 to A4 to A5
B1 to B2, B3 to B4 to B(1,2) to A
C1 to C2 to C3, C4 to C5 to C(1,2,3) to C6
to C7 to AB
D1 to D2 to D3 to ABC
E1 to E2, E3 to E4 to E5 to E(1,2) to ABCD

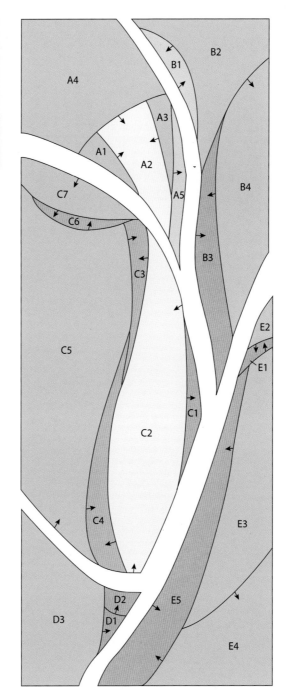

Corn curved-seam piecing diagram

Eggplant

# Eggplant
## *Straight Seams*

I've chosen a slimmer eggplant for the straight seam block and a more voluptuous one to piece with curves. In addition to the dark purple eggplants most often found in stores, there are streaky lavender eggplants and small white eggplants that look exactly like white chicken eggs.

The proposed quilt design uses both the eggplant block and the reverse, with the columns shifted in a brickwork pattern. Rectangles and squares are added to create a rectangular quilt.

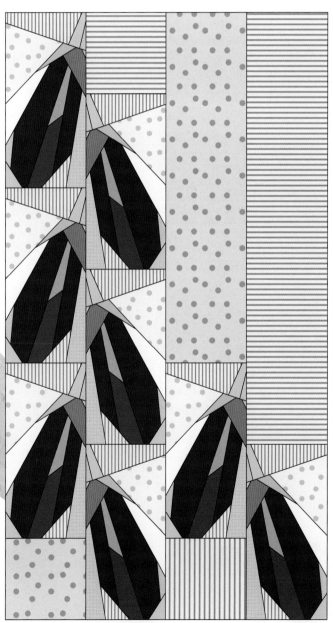

Eggplant straight-seam quilt design

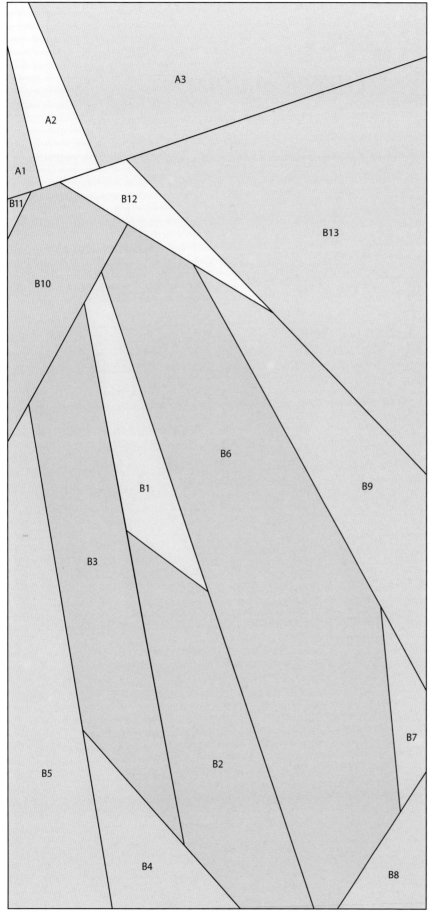

Eggplant straight-seam block
Enlarge this block 111% to a 10½" x 5" rectangle, see page 9.

If you could find just the right fabric, purple with a light highlight, you might be able to cut pieces B1, B2, B3 and B6 as one piece. Lacking that perfect fabric, choose a light highlight for B1, and darker purples for B2, B3 and B6.

The size suggested is the minimum practical sewing size. To make it easier, make it bigger. During construction press the seam allowance in the direction indicated by the arrows on the piecing diagram.

Sew:
A1 to A2 to A3
B1 to B2 to B3 to B4 to B5 to B6 to B7 to B8 to B9 to B10 to B11 to B12 to B13 to A

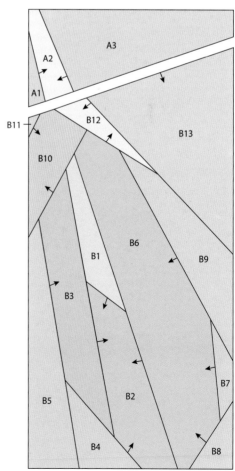

Eggplant straight-seam piecing diagram

# Eggplant
## Curved Seams

A few of the curved seams in this block are S-curves, that is, they are concave in one part and convex further on. You may find it easier in sewing S-curves to sew them in sections, sewing a section with the concave (clipped) part on top, stopping, removing the piece from the sewing machine, turning it over, then sewing the next concave section, with the next clips on top. I find it easier to sew curves when I can see the clips.

In this quilt design, I used four blocks in one row and four reverse blocks in the other.

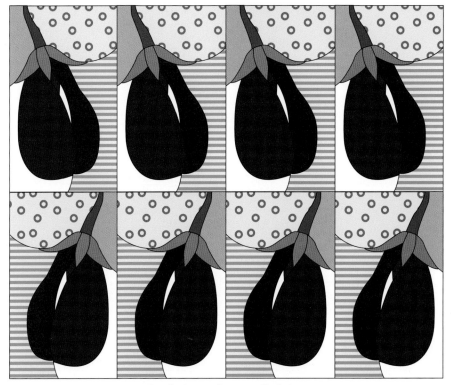

Eggplant curved-seam quilt design

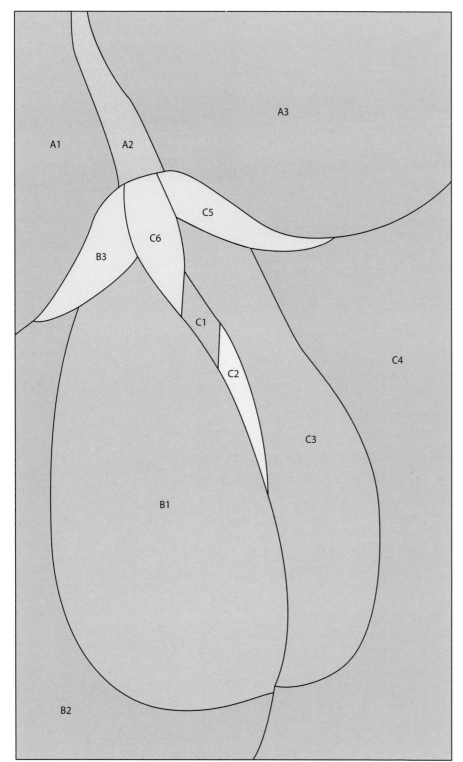

Eggplant curved-seam block
Enlarge this block 128% to a 10" x 6" rectangle, see page 9.

The size suggested is the minimum practical sewing size. To make it easier, make it bigger. During construction press the seam allowance in the direction indicated by the arrows on the piecing diagram.

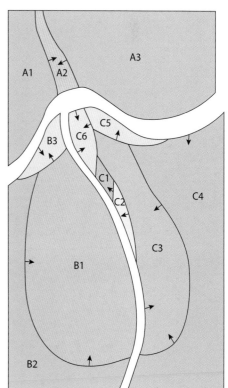

Eggplant curved-seam piecing diagram

Sew:
A1 to A2 to A3
B1 to B2 to B3
C1 to C2 to C3 to C4 to C5 to C6 to B to A

Leeks

# Leeks
## Straight Seams

The straight-seam block is very easy to piece with freezer paper. You might add a little fringe of thick white threads in the seam below the white base to make "roots."

*I love to look at the details of the patterns of growth of plants. The green leaves of leeks emerge from the white base in flat patterns exactly like the corner of a log cabin quilt block.*

Leek straight-seam quilt design

In the quilt design I have used pairs of blocks to form squares, then set the squares in pin-wheel patterns. The pinwheels at the upper left and lower right are made with the original block as drawn. The pinwheels at the upper right and lower left are made from the block reversed and used in pairs. This arrangement makes "mirror lines" vertically and horizontally through the center of the quilt.

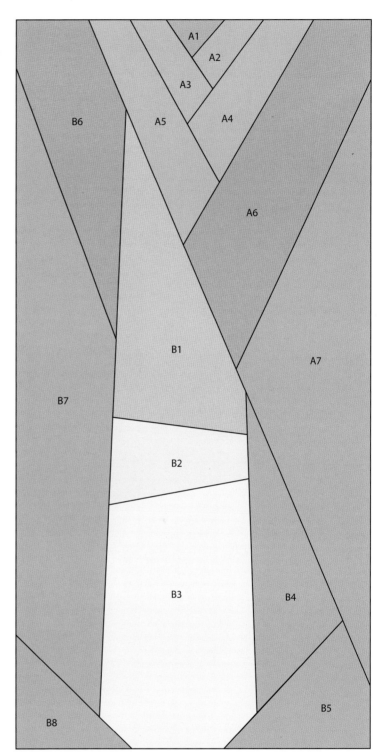

Leek straight-seam block
Enlarge this block 105% to an 8" x 4" rectangle, see page 9.

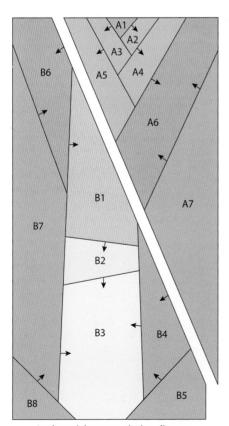

Leek straight-seam piecing diagram

Sew:
A1 to A2 to A3 to A4 to A5 to A6 to A7
B1 to B2 to B3 to B4 to B5
B6 to B7 to B(1,2,3,4,5) to B8 to A

The size suggested is the minimum practical sewing size. To make it easier, make it bigger. During construction press the seam allowance in the direction indicated by the arrows on the piecing diagram.

# Leeks

## Curved Seams

For the curved-seam block, I have included a little piece for "roots" which you might cut from a small stripe.

The quilt design uses both plain and reversed blocks, this time in columns. The top horizontal row of this quilt design is made from original blocks, first with the leaves at the top, then with the leaves at the bottom. This row might be used alone as a border design. The second horizontal row is made from four reversed blocks, starting with the leaves at the bottom.

Leek curved-seam quilt design

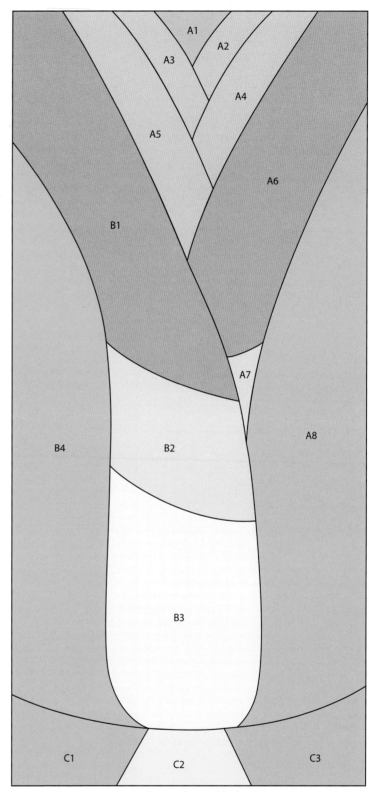

Leek curved-seam block
Enlarge this block 105% to a 8½" x 4" rectangle, see page 9.

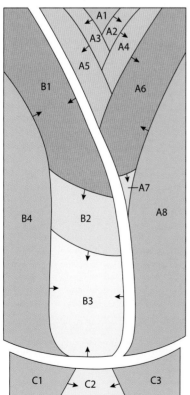

Leek curved-seam piecing diagram

Sew:
A1 to A2 to A3 to A4 to A5 to A6 to A7 to A8
B1 to B2 to B3 to B4 to A
C1 to C2 to C3 to AB

The size suggested is the minimum practical sewing size. To make it easier, make it bigger. During construction press the seam allowance in the direction indicated by the arrows.

# Lettuce

There are many varieties
of lettuces in addition
to the usual iceberg.
The range of different
greens in leaf lettuce
range from creamy yellow
to very pale green,
to bright or dark greens
and combinations
of green and red.

# Romaine Lettuce
## Straight Seams

Romaine is the leaf lettuce used in Caesar salads. The thick crunchy midribs are almost white in color, in contrast with the bright and dark greens of the leaves. If machine quilting this block, you might use a loose stipple pattern on the leaves to texture them.

Romaine lettuce straight-seam quilt design

In this quilt design, I have used both blocks and reverse blocks, and placed them right side up and upside down. By using several different fabrics in the background, it becomes part of the overall design, one of the advantages of piecing.

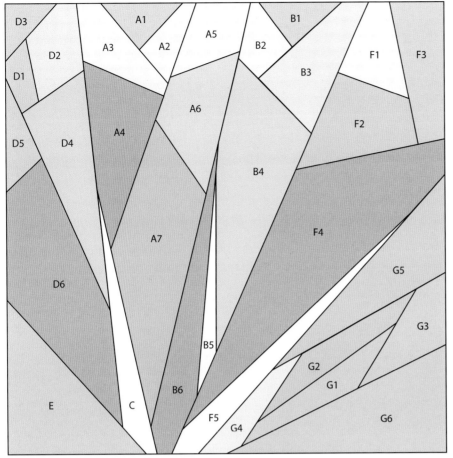

Romaine lettuce straight-seam block
Enlarge this block 213% to a 10" x 10" square, see page 9.

The size suggested is the minimum practical sewing size. To make it easier, make it bigger. During construction press the seam allowance in the direction indicated by the arrows on the piecing diagram.

Sew:
A1 to A2 to A3 to A4, A5 to A6 to A7 to A(1,2,3,4)
B1 to B2 to B3 to B4 to B5 to B6 to A to C
D1 to D2 to D3 to D4, D5 to D6 to D(1,2,3,4)
ABC to D to E
F1 to F2 to F3 to F4 to F5 to ABCDE
G1 to G2 to G3 to G4 to G5 to G6 to ABCDEF

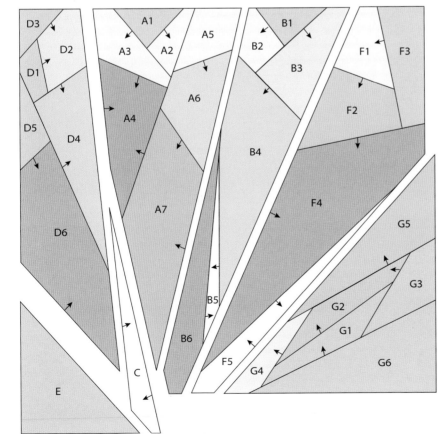

Romaine lettuce straight-seam piecing diagram

# Boston Lettuce
## Curved Seams

Boston lettuce is one of the head lettuce varieties. Rather than a loose cluster of leaves, they form tight heads, like a cabbage. Iceberg is another head lettuce variety. Lettuce leaves are much more delicate than cabbage. I've chosen to try to illustrate that by choosing gentle curves for the Boston lettuce, instead of the straight seams used in the cabbage block, page 42. The gentle curves, however, make this a much more difficult block to sew than the cabbage.

For the first quilt design, I have used the block as drawn (no reversed blocks). Half of the blocks have one background color scheme and half have the other. The blocks are then placed in pinwheels around a small square. The square is a "puzzle" piece. See Green Beans, page 25, for assembly of the pinwheels.

For the second quilt design, I have used one set of background fabrics in the lettuce block and a different set of background fabrics in the reversed blocks. Notice the mirror reflection down the center between the vertical rows.

Boston lettuce curved-seam quilt designs

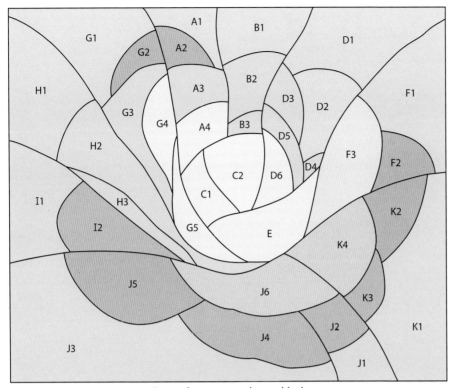

Boston lettuce curved-seam block
Enlarge this block 256% to a 10" x 12" rectangle, see page 9.

The size suggested is the minimum practical sewing size. To make it easier, make it bigger. During construction press the seam allowance in the direction indicated by the arrows on the piecing diagram.

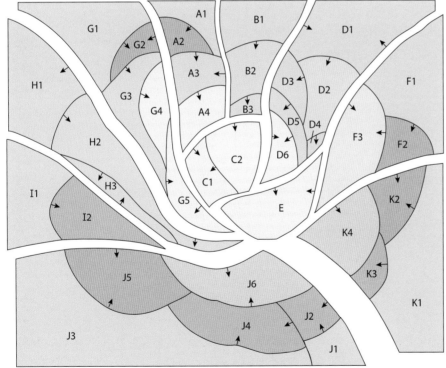

Boston lettuce curved-seam piecing diagram

Sew:
A1 to A2 to A3 to A4
B1 to B2 to B3 to A
C1 to C2 to AB
D1 to D2 to D3 to D4 to D5 to D6 to ABC
ABCD to E
F1 to F2 to F3 to ABCDE
G1 to G2 to G3 to G4 to G5 to ABCDEF
H1 to H2 to H3 to ABCDEFG
I1 to I2 to ABCDEFGH
K1 to K2 to K3 to K4
J1 to J2, J3 to J4 to J5 to J(1,2) to J6 to K
ABCDEFGHI to JK

# Onions

Onions may be white, yellow, tan, or red, giving you many possible colors to use. Try to find a fabric with a swirled design to add detail to the bulb.

# Onions
## *Straight Seams*

Onions may be white, yellow, tan, or red, giving you many possible fabrics from which to choose. Try to find a fabric with a linear pattern to add detail to the bulb.

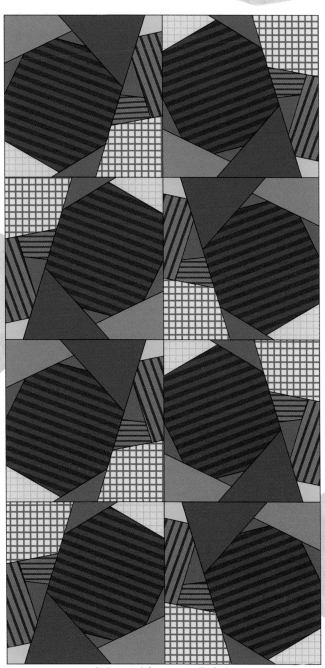

This quilt layout uses the block as drawn and the reversed block. The color scheme is the same for all the blocks. Notice how much more interesting the quilt design is with different colors in the background spaces.

Onion straight-seam quilt design

Use a stripe for the top A1 and A3. Draw the direction of the stripe on the dull side of the freezer paper pattern as an aid in placing the freezer paper at the right angle on the fabric. This is one of the simplest blocks in the book to piece.

The size suggested is the minimum practical sewing size. To make it easier, make it bigger. During construction press the seam allowance in the direction indicated by the arrows on the piecing diagram.

Sew:
A1 to A2 to A3 to A4 to A5
B1 to B2 to B3 to B4 to B5 to B6 to B7 to A

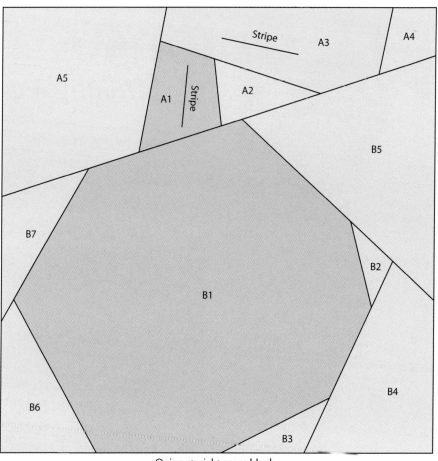

Onion straight-seam block
Enlarge this block 108% to a 5" x 5" square, see page 9.

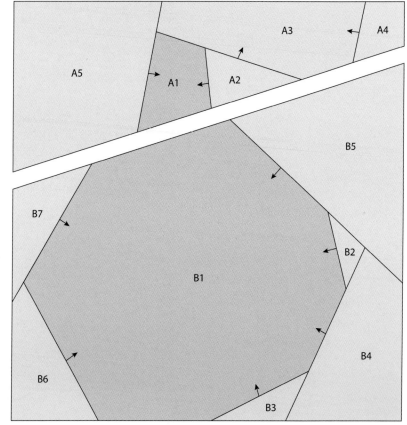

Onion straight-seam piecing diagram

# Onions
## *Curved Seams*

Here's another curved-seam design that seems Art Nouveau in style. It is a much more difficult block to piece than the straight-seam onion block.

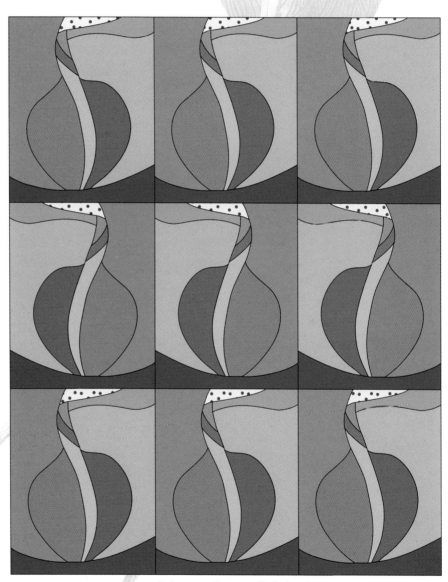

Onion curved-seam quilt design

Here's a quilt of nine blocks. The three blocks in the center row use the block as drawn. The six blocks making the top and bottom rows are reverses of the onion block as drawn. The top of the onion is at the top in each case. Notice the sinuous vertical pattern that develops down the center of each column.

If this block was enlarged twice the minimum size to 20" x 16" (382%), it would make a nice small wallhanging all by itself. You could then use the quilting stitches, either by hand or machine, to add the striped veins you see in the real onion, and to add roots on piece E.

The size suggested is the minimum practical sewing size. To make it easier, make it bigger. During construction press the seam allowance in the direction indicated by the arrows on the piecing diagram.

Sew:
A1 to A2 to A3
B1 to B2 to B3 to A to C
D1 to D2 to ABC
ABCD to E

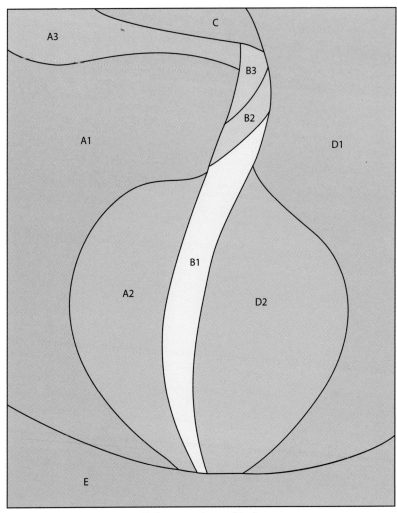

Onion curved-seam block
Enlarge this block 192% to a 10" x 8" rectangle, see page 9.

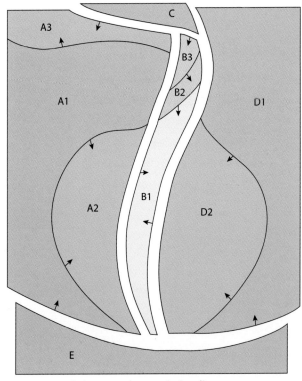

Onion curved-seam piecing diagram

Peas

# Peas
## Straight Seams

Only eight pieces! Make the five background pieces each a different color and the sepals, pieces 8 and 6, a slightly darker green than the pod. If you get really lucky, you might find a large polka dot you could fussy-cut for piece 1 to make peas in the pod.

Piecing small circles is an impossible task, so I've had to be creative to show the peas. The straight-seam block is very easy to sew, the curved-seam block more difficult.

Add the "peas" when quilting the pod, either by hand or machine. I really like this quilt design. It is composed of a repeated horizontal row. The row uses both the original block as drawn and the reversed block, some blocks with the sepals at the top, some with the sepals at the bottom.

Pea straight-seam quilt design

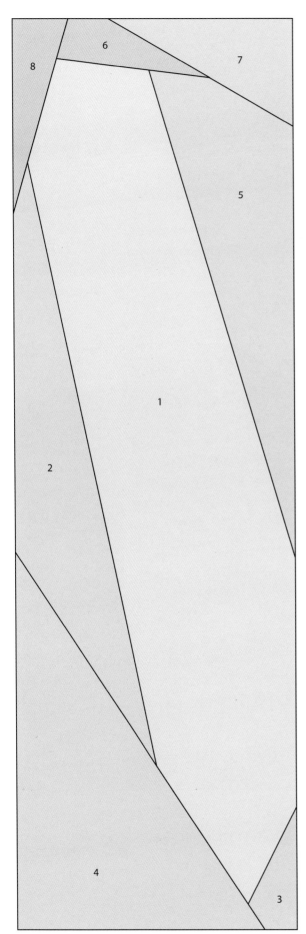

Pea straight-seam block
This block is actual size, a 9½" x 3" rectangle.

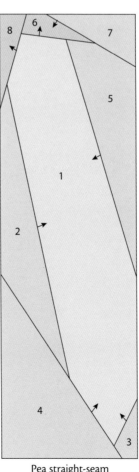

Pea straight-seam
piecing diagram

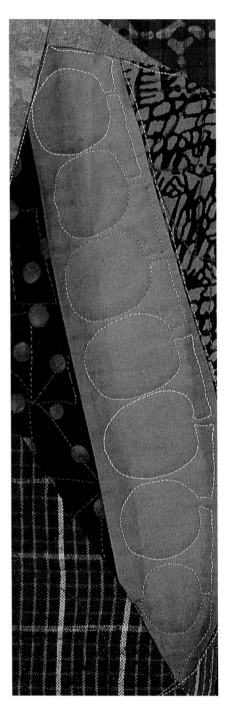

The size suggested is the minimum practical sewing size. To make it easier, make it bigger. During construction press the seam allowance in the direction indicated by the arrows on the piecing diagram.

Sew:
1 to 2 to 3 to 4 to 5 to 6 to 7 to 8

# Peas
## Curved Seams

The "peas" in the open pod could be made in different ways. Piece A(1,2,3,4,5,6,7,8) can be cut as a single fabric and the peas drawn in when the quilting is added. Or A1 through A8 can be cut as separate pieces (of slightly different fabrics) and sewn with templates. Or Pieces A1 through A8 can be foundation pieced on a freezer-paper template A(1,2,3,4,5,6,7,8). Or cut a single piece of fabric for A(1,2,3,4,5,6,7,8) and appliqué individual peas on it, before piecing on A 9 and A10.

Or find a single piece of printed fabric with a row of dots or beads from which piece A(1,2,3,4,5,6,7,8) could be fussy-cut (there is one I can think of that would work).

The quilt design is composed of four pinwheels of four blocks each: the pinwheels at the upper right and the lower left made of the block as originally drawn; the pinwheels at the upper left and lower right of the reversed block. This makes a mirror line through the center of the quilt both vertically and horizontally.

Pea curved-seam quilt design

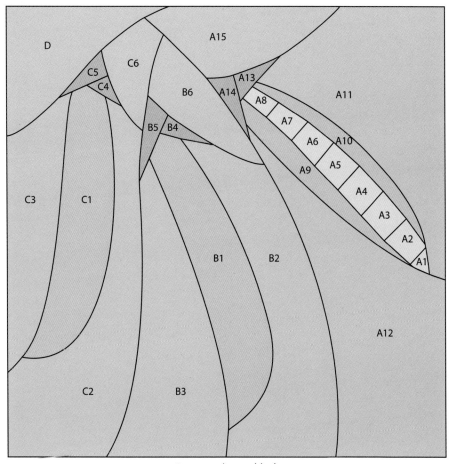

Pea curved-seam block
Enlarge this block 213% to a 10" x 10" square, see page 9.

The size suggested is the minimum practical sewing size. To make it easier, make it bigger. During construction press the seam allowance in the direction indicated by the arrows on the piecing diagram.

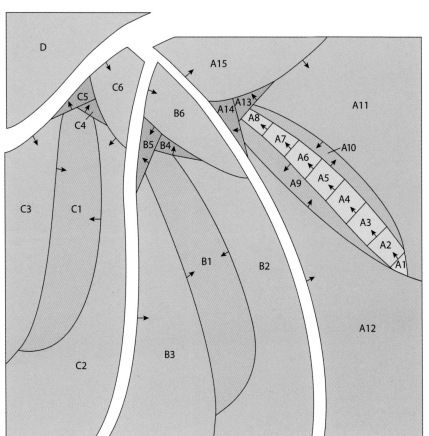

Pea curved-seam piecing diagram

Sew:
A1 to A2 to A3 to A4 to A5 to S6 to A7 to A8 to make the peas in the open pod, or use a single piece of fabric for A(1,2,3,4,5,6,7,8). A(1,2,3,4,5,6,7,8) to A9 to A10 to A11 to A12 to A13, to A14 to A15
B1 to B2 to B3 to B4 to B5 to B6
C1 to C2 to C3 to C4 to C5 to C6
C to B to A to D

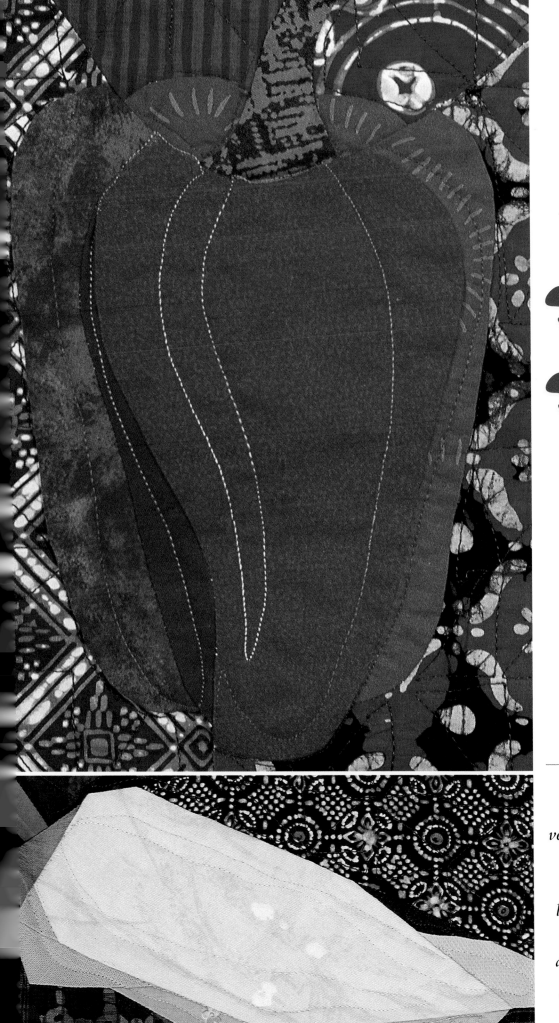

# Peppers

Peppers are available in more colors than any other vegetable I can think of: green, red, yellow, orange, purple, chocolate hues, white, and light or dark shades of each. The shapes and sizes are almost as varied. I've chosen just a few for this chapter.

# Italian Peppers
## Straight Seams

Usually pale green, sometimes yellow or red, the Italian-type pepper has a more slender shape than some sweet peppers. The fruit of the pepper in this straight-seam block, Pieces A2, A3, A4, B1, C2, and C3 might each be cut from a slightly different fabric to shade and round the form and give it more interest. Pieces D2, E2, and E3 make the cap and stem.

Slipping the vertical columns of blocks in a brickwork pattern by adding the plain rectangles as shown here is easy to sew. The resulting design is much more interesting than a more standard set.

Italian pepper straight-seam quilt design

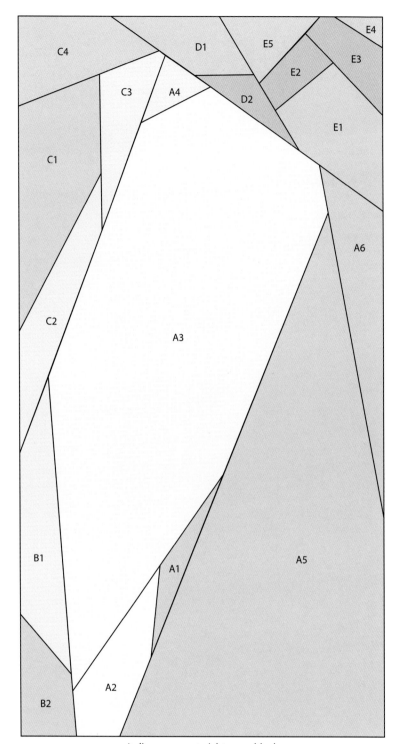

Italian pepper straight-seam block
Enlarge this block 127% to a 9½" x 5" rectangle, see page 9.

The size suggested is the minimum practical sewing size. To make it easier, make it bigger. During construction press the seam allowance in the direction indicated by the arrows on the piecing diagram.

Sew:
A1 to A2 to A3 to A4 to A5 to A6
B1 to B2 to A
C1 to C2 to C3 to C4 to AB
D1 to D2
E1 to E2 to E3 to E4 to E5 to D
ABC to DE

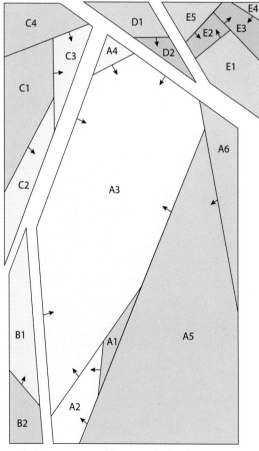

Italian pepper straight-seam piecing diagram

# Ristra Peppers
## *Straight Seams*

Here's a chance to make a ristra, a string of dried peppers to hang in your kitchen. The block is a parallelogram. Piece B7 will become the stem of Pepper A1 in the next block when a string of blocks are joined together. The addition of a triangle to the top and bottom of the string turns it into a long rectangle for ease in inserting it into a quilt or for making a small wallhanging or table runner.

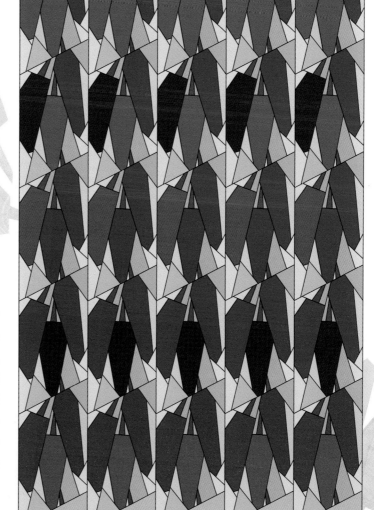

Ristra straight-seam quilt design

The pepper strings can be used as an all-over pattern as in the quilt design shown, or a single string can be used as a border element. Notice how the individual blocks don't stand out; they disappear as several blocks are joined together. If I had used a rectangle for the block shape, rather than slanting the top and bottom edges of the block, you could pick out the individual blocks more easily.

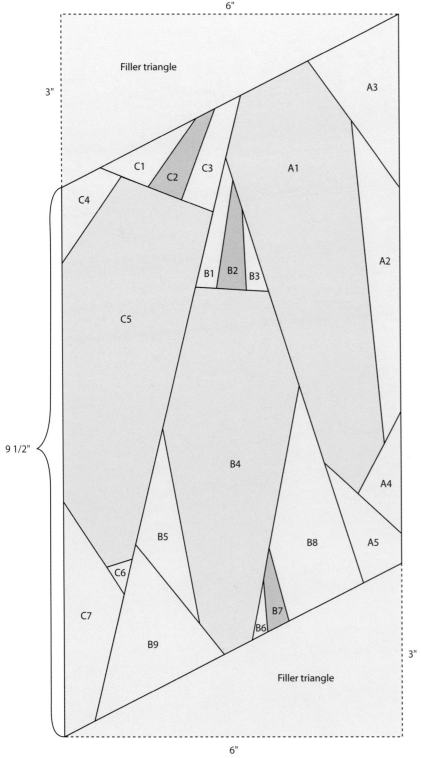

6"

Filler triangle

3"

C1  C2  C3

C4

A3

A1

A2

B1  B2  B3

C5

B4

A4

B5

A5

C6

B8

C7

B7

B9  B6

3"

Filler triangle

9 1/2"

6"

Ristra straight-seam block
Enlarge this block 165% to a parallelogram 9½" high, see page 9.

The size suggested is the minimum practical sewing size. To make it easier, make it bigger. During construction press the seam allowance in the direction indicated by the arrows on the piecing diagram.

Sew:
A1 to A2 to A3 to A4 to A5
B1 to B2 to B3 to B4 to B5
B6 to B7 to B8 to B(1,2,3,4,5) to B9 to A
C1 to C2 to C3
C4 to C5 to C(1,2,3) to C6 to C7 to AB

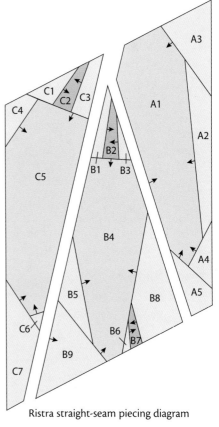

Ristra straight-seam piecing diagram

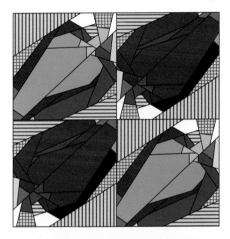

# Bell Pepper
## *Straight Seams*

The variety of colors in bell peppers is amazing. Wouldn't it be fun to make a quilt with all of them: red, orange, yellow, green, purple, ivory, and chocolate?

Here are a number of four-block quilt designs. They would make nice, small wall hangings, although you may want to enlarge the blocks to 15" on a side for ease of sewing. Any of these layouts could be expanded, of course, to a full-size bed quilt.

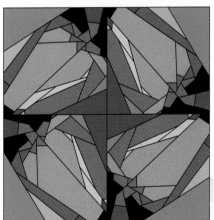

Bell pepper straight-seam quilt designs

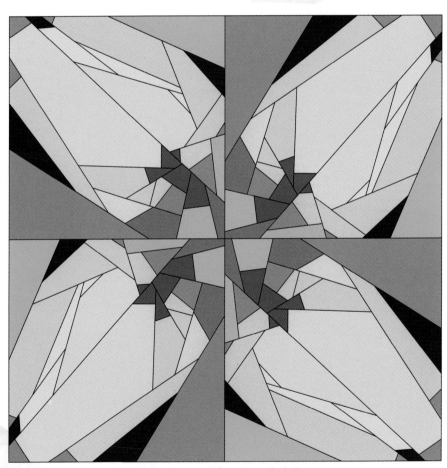

Bell pepper straight-seam quilt design

The top quilt design shows two red peppers with a lot of diagonal motion. The lower design, a pinwheel of peppers, forms a simple star at the center.

A pinwheel of peppers with a different corner of the block at the center of the pinwheel. Many different background fabrics, especially in the little background pieces at the center of the pinwheel, will make a fascinating quilt.

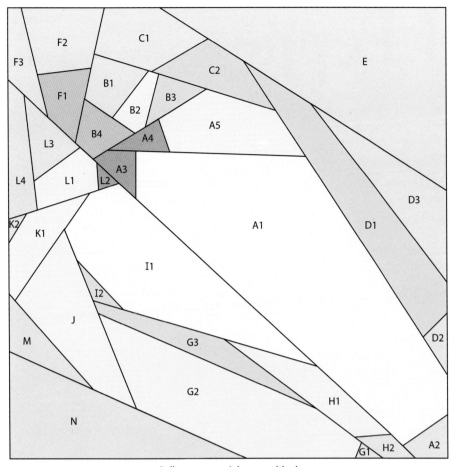

Bell pepper straight-seam block
Enlarge this block 213% to a 10" x 10" square, see page 9.

This straight-seam block breaks the pepper into many pieces to show off the folds and shadows seen on this shiny fruit. Because of the number of pieces, this will be a much more time-consuming block to make than either the Italian pepper block or the ristra block.

The size suggested is the minimum practical sewing size. To make it easier, make it bigger. During construction press the seam allowance in the direction indicated by the arrows on the piecing diagram.

Sew:
A1 to A2 to A3, A4 to A5 to A(1,2,3)
B1 to B2 to B3 to B4 to A
C1 to C2 to AB
D1 to D2 to D3 to ABC to E
F1 to F2 to F3 to ABCDE
G1 to G2 to G3
H1 to H2 to G
I1 to I2 to GH to J to K1 to K2
L1 to L2 to L3 to L4 to GHIJK to M to N
to ABCDE

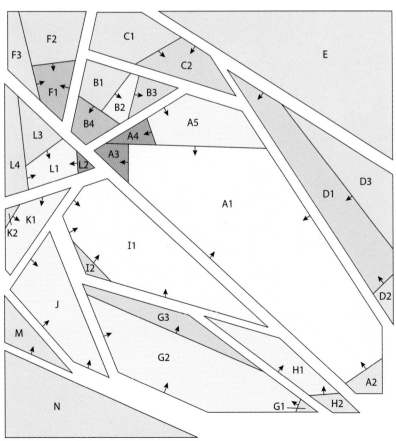

Bell pepper straight-seam piecing diagram

# Bell Pepper
## *Curved Seams*

The curved-seam version of the bell pepper has fewer templates than the previous straight-seam version. The look of this block, because of the curves, is much different as well. Curves are slower to sew than straight seams. If you haven't done much curved-seam piecing this block may take you as long to sew as the straight-seam version.

This quilt uses the peppers as drawn and the reverse block. A wavy motion develops between the rows.

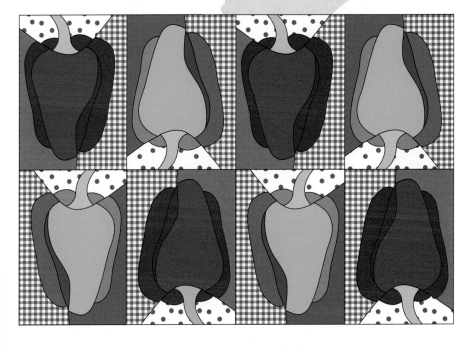

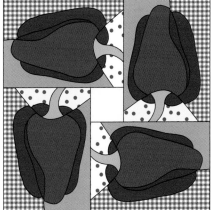

A pinwheel of peppers around a center square. See Green Beans, page 25, to assemble this group. Notice how the stems flow almost in a circle.

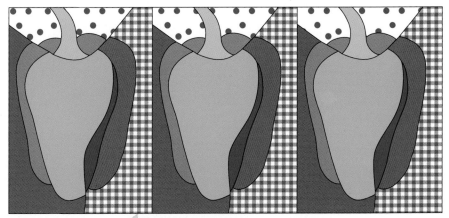

Bell pepper curved-seam quilt designs

Three peppers in a row — maybe a border at the ends of a table runner or on kitchen curtains.

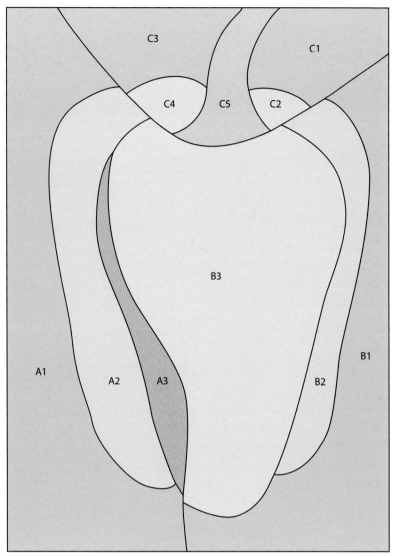

Bell pepper curved-seam block
Enlarge this block 158% to a 9" x 6½" rectangle, see page 9.

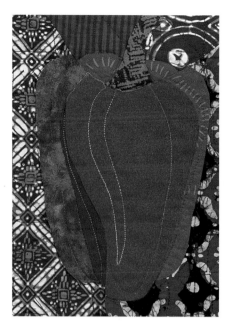

The size suggested is the minimum practical sewing size. To make it easier, make it bigger. During construction press the seam allowance in the direction indicated by the arrows on the piecing diagram.

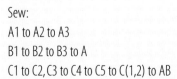

Sew:
A1 to A2 to A3
B1 to B2 to B3 to A
C1 to C2, C3 to C4 to C5 to C(1,2) to AB

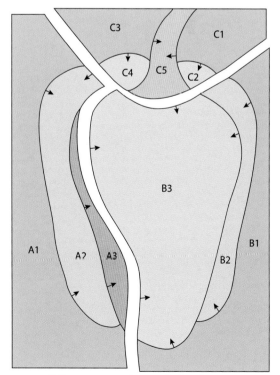

Bell pepper curved-seam piecing diagram

# Potatoes

*Potatoes can be found with skins of gold, brown, tan, white, cream, and even purple. Some of them are smooth, some much rougher.*

# Potatoes
## *Straight Seams*

Potatoes have "eyes," the little dents in the surface where the buds for next year's sprouts hide. I can't pass up this name when choosing fabrics, and have fussy-cut printed eyes from a doll fabric for my potatoes. Look also at printed animal or cowboy fabrics for potato eyes.

If you want to eliminate piecing the eyes, add those little bits to the adjacent potato piece. Piece the blocks. Then, when quilting the potatoes, put heavy cotton ties at the places where you want eyes. Trim the ends of the ties short so they don't look like sprouting potatoes.

In the quilt design, notice that I have made piece C, a background piece, a much lighter color to bring out the narrow pinwheels. This quilt layout is the same symmetry pattern I have used before in the curved-seam pea quilt, and the straight-seam leek quilt. To make this quilt design you will need eight blocks as originally drawn and eight reverse blocks. For additional variety, you might make the remaining background pieces of the four blocks in the center slightly lighter or darker than the backgrounds of the outer blocks.

Potato straight-seam quilt design

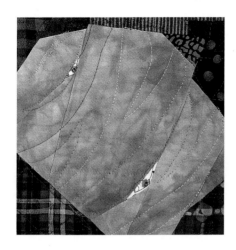

The size suggested is the minimum practical sewing size. To make it easier, make it bigger. During construction press the seam allowance in the direction indicated by the arrows on the piecing diagram.

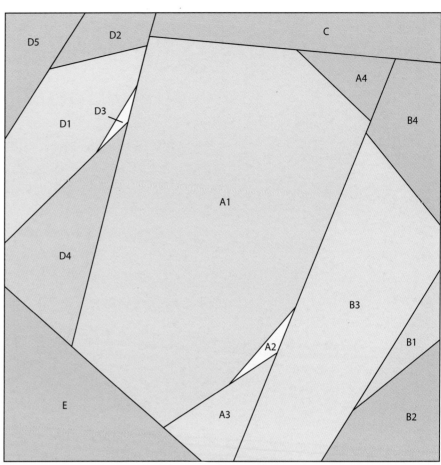

Potato straight-seam block
Enlarge this block 128% to a 6" x 6" square, see page 9.

Sew:
A1 to A2 to A3 to A4
B1 to B2 to B3 to B4 to A to C
D1 to D2 to D3 to D4 to D5 to ABC to E

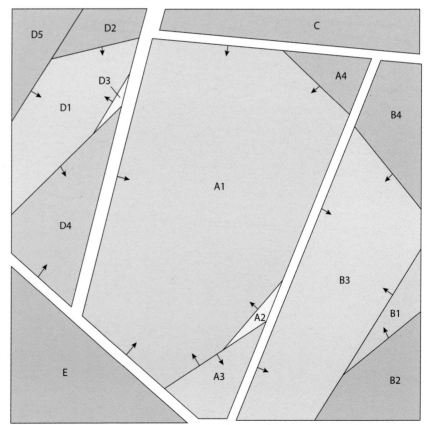

Potato straight-seam piecing diagram

# Potatoes
## Curved Seams

In the quilt design, notice how section B in each block suggests an interlocking ring pattern. This might be emphasized by making B3 and B4 distinctly different from the other background pieces; i.e., very much lighter or darker, or a different hue or printed pattern. This quilt design contains eight blocks as originally drawn and eight reverses.

Potato curved-seam quilt design

I found it easier to reverse appliqué the eyes, pieces B1 and C1, to the potato pieces, B2 and C2, by hand before starting the piecing. (Reverse appliqué makes the eyes go in like dents, as they really do. Appliqué would put them on top of the potato surface.)

The size suggested is the minimum practical sewing size. To make it easier, make it bigger. During construction press the seam allowance in the direction indicated by the arrows on the piecing diagram.

Sew:
Reverse appliqué B1 to B2 and C1 to C2
A1 to A2 to A3
B(1,2) to B3 to B4 to A
C(1,2) to C3 to C4 to AB

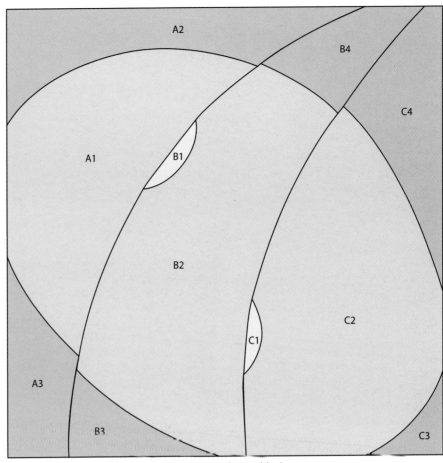

Potato curved-seam block
Enlarge this block 128% to a 6" x 6" square, see page 9.

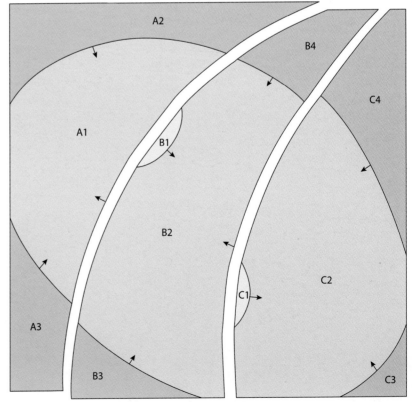

Potato curved-seam piecing diagram

Pumpkin

# Pumpkin
## Straight and Inset Corner Seams

The pumpkin is sewn with a combination of straight seams and inset corner seams that are clipped at the pivot points. There is a Y seam at the dot. I like the look of round shapes drawn with angled lines.

I really do like pinwheel patterns. Here's another one. Because the pumpkin block is rectangular rather than a square, this pinwheel requires the addition of a little inset square, whose dimensions are the difference between the length and width of the block, in this case, 1". See Green Beans, page 25, for instruction on sewing the blocks together.

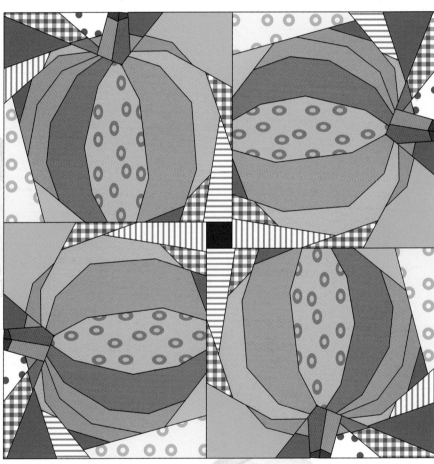

Pumpkin quilt design

If you like the pinwheel idea but don't want to inset the square, add to the top or bottom of the pumpkin block to make the pieced block into a square.

The size suggested is the minimum practical
sewing size. To make it easier, make it bigger.
During construction press the seam allowance
in the direction indicated by the arrows on
the piecing diagram.

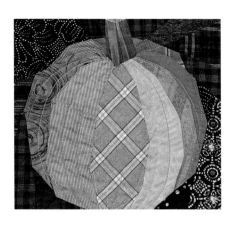

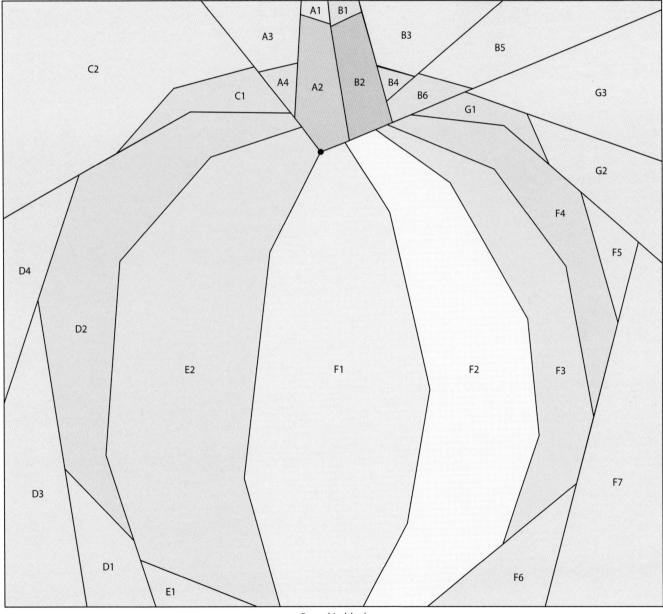

Pumpkin block
Enlarge this block 126% to an 8" x 9" rectangle, see page 9.

Sew:
A1 to A2, A3 to A4 to A(1,2)
B1 to B2, B3 to B4, B5 to B6 to B(3,4)
to B(1,2) to A
C1 to C2
D1 to D2 to D3 to D4 to C
E1 to E2 to CD
F1 to F2 to F3 to F4 to F5 to F6 to F7
G1 to G2 to G3 to F
AB to CDE, backstitching at •
AB to FG, backstitching at •
CDE to FG, backstitching at •

For all of the pieces that are simple straight seams, leave the freezer paper on the back of the fabric and sew along the edge. For the inset corner seams (C1 to C2, C to D, D to E, F1 to F2 to F3 to F4, G to F, and F to E), follow the directions in sewing inset corners, below.

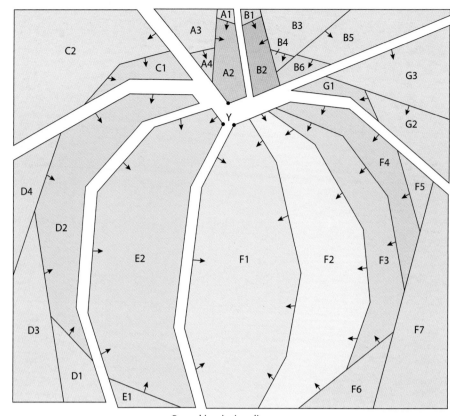

Pumpkin piecing diagram

## SEWING INSET CORNERS

· Cut seam allowances with ruler and rotary cutter as in straight-seam piecing.
· Be careful at inner corners.

· Trace around edge of freezer paper.
· Mark tics in seam allowance.
· Clip inner corners, almost all the way to the seam (leave just a thread or two).
· Remove freezer paper. Shorten stitch length to 1.5.
· Set "needle down" if available.
· Match (0) dots and (1) dots.
· Sew with clipped (concave) piece on top.
· Start sewing at edge of fabric and sew to (1).
· Needle down in (1).
· Raise presser foot.

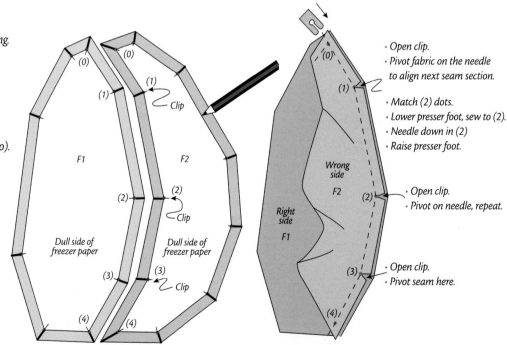

· Open clip.
· Pivot fabric on the needle to align next seam section.

· Match (2) dots.
· Lower presser foot, sew to (2).
· Needle down in (2).
· Raise presser foot.

· Open clip.
· Pivot on needle, repeat.

· Open clip.
· Pivot seam here.

# Squash

One could make a whole book of pieced designs from the shapes and colors of squash. I've chosen a Buttercup squash, one of my personal favorites for flavor.

# Squash
## Curved Seams

The buttercup squash has a nice pattern with a rough raised band on the side of the squash where the flower was, and a sturdy stem on the opposite side.

Here are two blocks, one looking at the blossom end with lots of detailed piecing, and a much simpler one at the stem end.

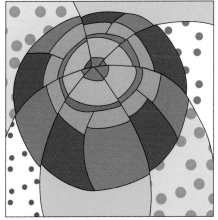

Buttercup squash blossom end

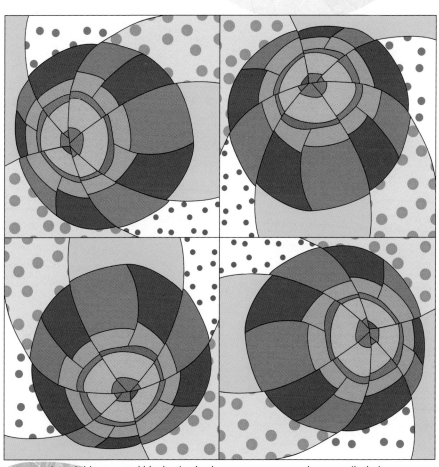

Squash blossom end block, pinwheel arrangement, curved-seam quilt design

Notice the suggestion of a large circle in the center of the quilt, under the squashes.

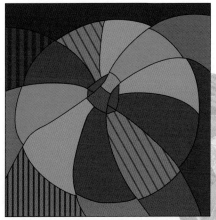

Buttercup squash stem end

A squash quilt using both blossom end and stem end blocks. I've used earthy colors as backgrounds, but have added some blues and purples, as well.

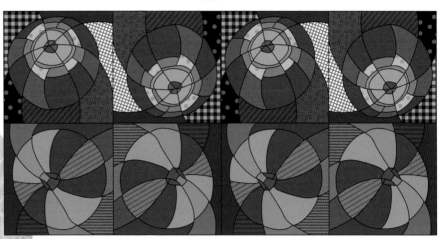

Squash stem and blossom end quilt design

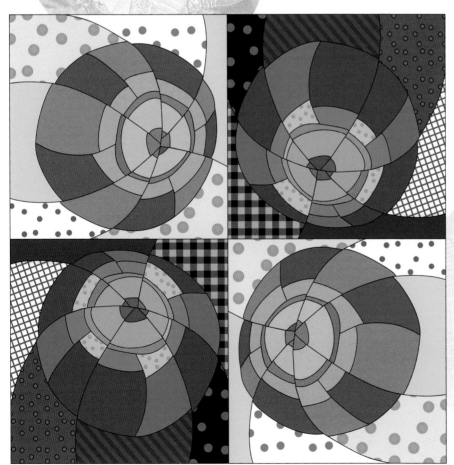

Squash blossom end block, pinwheel arrangement, curved-seam quilt design

In this second design, I've made two green squashes and two orange ones, which makes this pinwheel less prominent.

Piece 1 in each section is light brown in color, piece 2 a paler version of the main color, and piece 3 a raised rough corky ring. I've pressed both seam allowances under the ring to raise it up. You may want to trim the seam allowances after you have sewn the seam between pieces 2 and 3 before you add pieces 4 and 6. This block would be equally effective larger than the minimum size suggested, and easier to sew.

The size suggested is the minimum practical sewing size. To make it easier, make it bigger. During construction press the seam allowance in the direction indicated by the arrows on the piecing diagram.

Sew:
A1 to A2 to A3 to A4 to A5 to A6
B1 to B2 to B3, B4 to B5,
B6 to B7 to B(4,5) to B(1,2,3) to B8 to A
C1 to C2 to C3, C4 to C5,
C6 to C7 to C(4,5) to C(1,2,3) to C8 to AB
D1 to D2 to D3, D4 to D5,
D6 to D7 to D(4,5) to D(1,2,3) to D8
E1 to E2 to E3, E4 to E5,
E6 to E7 to E(4,5) to E(1,2,3) to E8 to D
F1 to F2 to F3 to F4 to F5 to F6 to DE to ABC

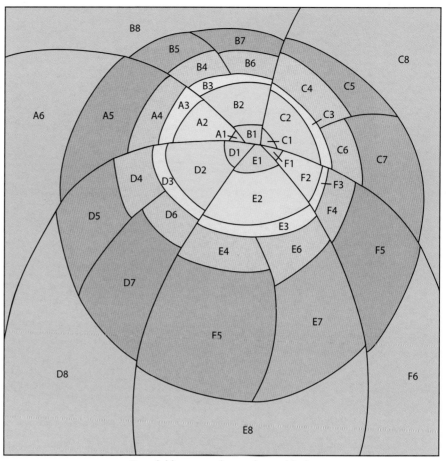

Squash blossom end curved-seam block
Enlarge this block 181% to an 8½" x 8½" square, see page 9.

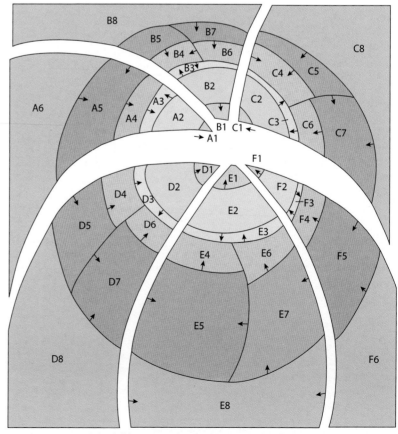

Squash blossom end curved-seam piecing diagram

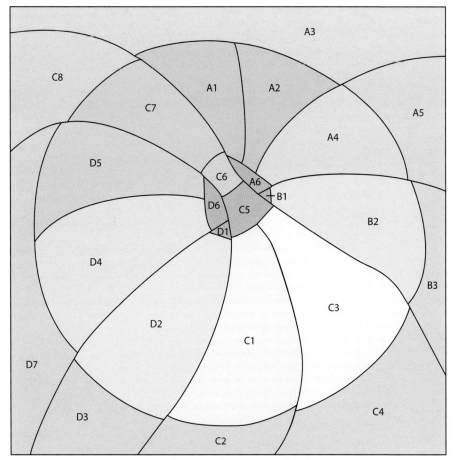

Squash stem end curved-seam block
Enlarge this block 181% to an 8½" x 8½" square, see page 9.

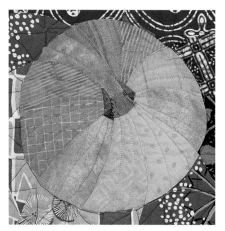

A much simpler block to sew than the previous one. Press the seam allowances as shown to pop up the stem. This squash is often subtly striped, with the stripes radiating out from the stem. If you choose to use striped fabric, mark the direction you want the stripes to go on the dull side of the freezer paper as an aid in placing the paper pieces on the back of the fabric in the right direction.

The size suggested is the minimum practical sewing size. To make it easier, make it bigger. During construction press the seam allowance in the direction indicated by the arrows on the piecing diagram.

Sew:
A1 to A2 to A3, A4 to A5 to A(1,2,3) to A6
B1 to B2 to B3 to A
C1 to C2,
C3 to C4 to C(1,2) to C5 to C6 to C7 to C8 to AB
D1 to D2 to D3,
D4 to D5 to D6 to D7 to D(1,2,3) to ABC

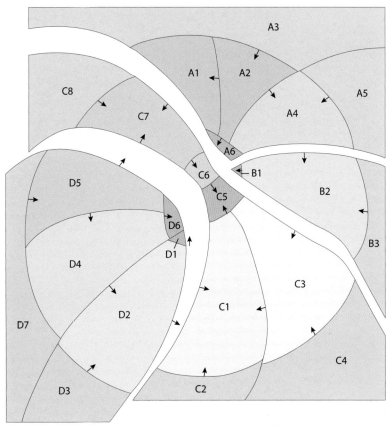

Squash stem end curved-seam piecing diagram

Tomatoes

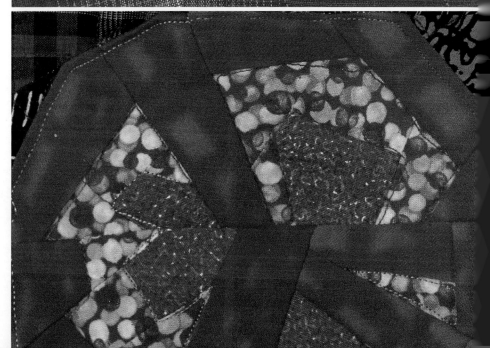

The pinnacle of many home vegetable gardens is the ripening of the first real red tomato. Homegrown tomatoes ripened on the vine and warm from the sun are a totally different

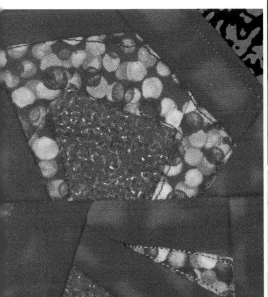

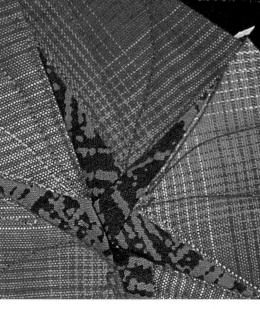

experience than any from a store, especially if you have nurtured the plants from seed to seedling anticipating the arrival of warm spring weather.

# Tomato
## *Straight Seams*

Pore through your seed catalogs and you will be amazed at the number of different colors of ripe tomatoes. I've made three blocks in this set, a tomato from the top, one from the side and a mouthwatering tomato slice.

I used a large-scale ombre plaid shaded from red to yellow for these tomatoes, fussy-cutting the fabric to make the tomatoes gleam.

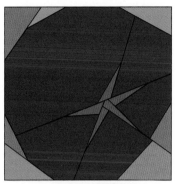

Tomato top view

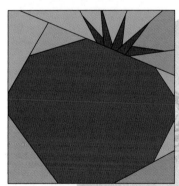

Tomato side view

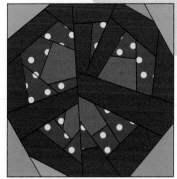

Tomato slice

Side view tomatoes (plus one slice) with rows of blocks as drawn and rows of reversed blocks.

Top views, side views, and slices scattered at random with some blocks reversed.

Tomato straight-seam quilt designs

All of these straight-seam blocks are 6" squares. Just one block might be pieced into a placemat, or several as a border on a curtain. You could space out the pieced tomato blocks in checkerboard fashion with 6" squares of gingham fabric to make a tablecloth or runner.

At 6" per block, this quilt design will be 42" x 36". How about adding a lettuce block border?

The many varieties of ripe tomato colors

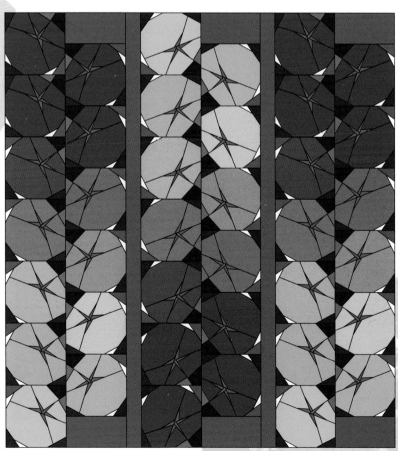

Just one of these three panels would make a nice wall hanging.

A raceme of cherry tomatoes slowly ripening

The size suggested is the minimum practical sewing size. To make it easier, make it bigger. During construction press the seam allowance in the direction indicated by the arrows on the piecing diagram.

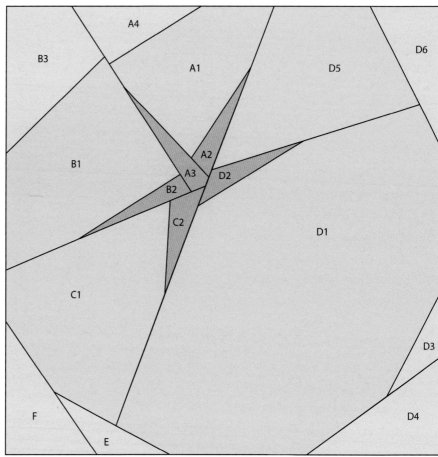

Tomato straight-seam top view block
Enlarge this block 128% to a 6" x 6" square, see page 9.

Sew:
A1 to A2 to A3 to A4
B1 to B2 to B3 to A
C1 to C2 to AB
D1 to D2 to D3 to D4 to D5 to D6 to
ABC to E to F

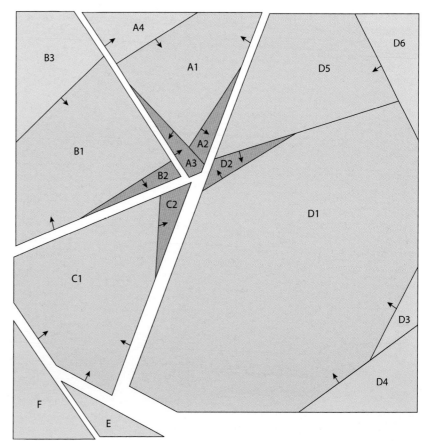

Tomato straight-seam top view piecing diagram

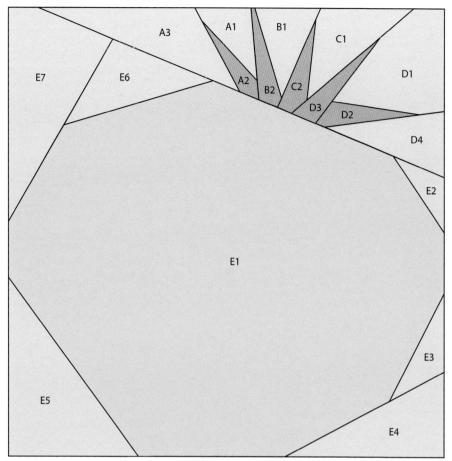

The size suggested is the minimum practical sewing size. To make it easier, make it bigger. During construction press the seam allowance in the direction indicated by the arrows on the piecing diagram.

Tomato straight-seam side view block
Enlarge this block 128% to a 6" x 6" square, see page 9.

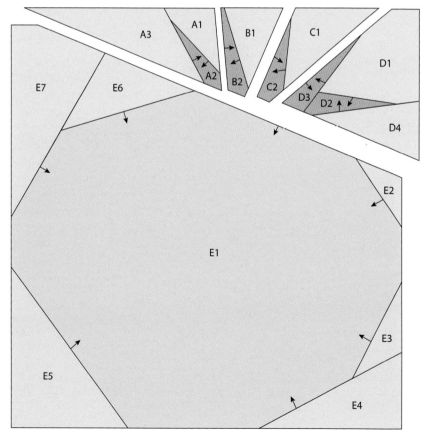

Sew:
A1 to A2 to A3
B1 to B2 to A
C1 to C2 to AB
D1 to D2 to D3 to D4 to ABC
E1 to E2 to E3 to E4 to E5 to E6 to E7 to ABCD

Tomato straight-seam side view piecing diagram

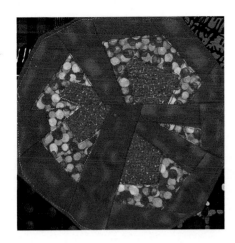

The size suggested is the minimum practical sewing size. To make it easier, make it bigger. During construction press the seam allowance in the direction indicated by the arrows on the piecing diagram.

Find a dotty print or calico for the tomato seed cavities, pieces A2, A3, A4, B2, B3, B4, B5, C1, D2, D3, E2, E3, F1, and solid fabrics for the rest of the tomato. The hunt for the perfect fabric is half the fun.

Sew:
A1 to A2 to A3 to A4 to A5 to A6 to A7 to A8
B1 to B2 to B3 to B4 to B5 to B6 to B7 to B8 to
B9 to A
C1 to C2
D1 to D2 to D3 to D4 to D5 to D6 to C
E1 to E2 to E3 to E4 to E5 to E6 to E7 to E8
F1 to F2 to F3 to E to CD to AB

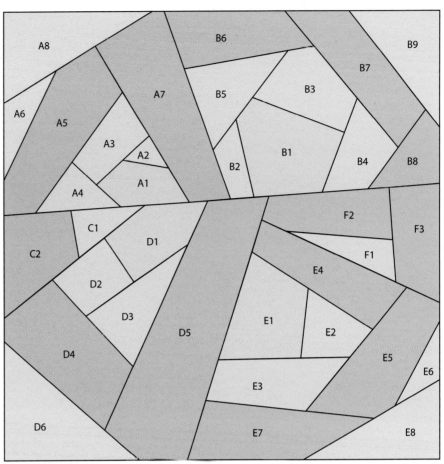

Tomato straight-seam slice block
Enlarge this block 128% to a 6" x 6" square, see page 9.

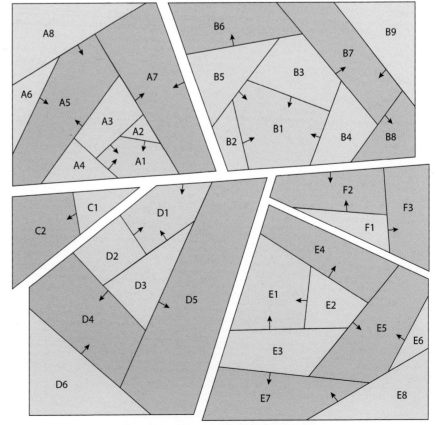

Tomato straight-seam slice piecing diagram

# Tomato
## Curved Seams

Here's another pair of tomato blocks, this time sewn with curved seams. The sepals (little green leaves at the top) can be sewn with templates in the ordinary way, or they could be added as either flip-and-sew elements, or as folded flaps, see page 122.

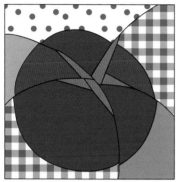

Tomato top view

Tomato side view with a highlight

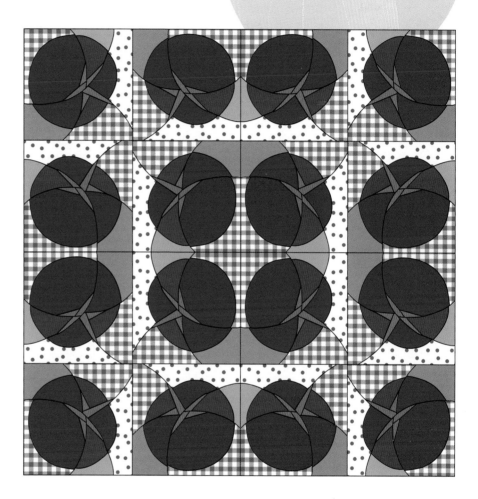

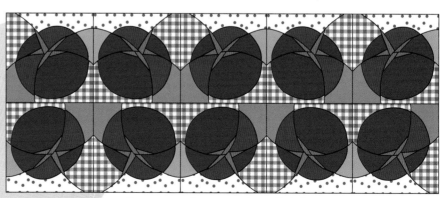

Tomato curved-seam top view quilt designs

Notice how interesting these quilt designs become with several different background fabrics used in the same block.

Tomato curved-seam top and side view quilt design

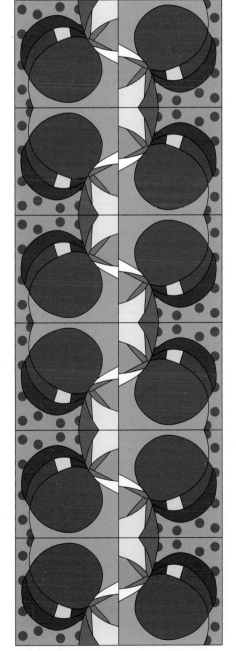

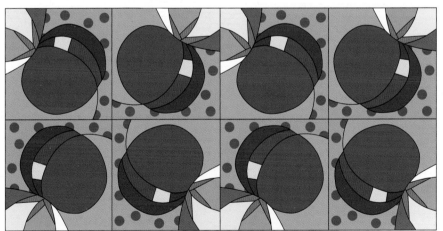

Tomato curved-seam side view quilt designs

The charm of using different fabrics in each of the background pieces really shows in these quilt examples. I've tried not to overwhelm the tomato images with intense colors in the background. Some of these quilts use reversed blocks as well as the block as drawn.

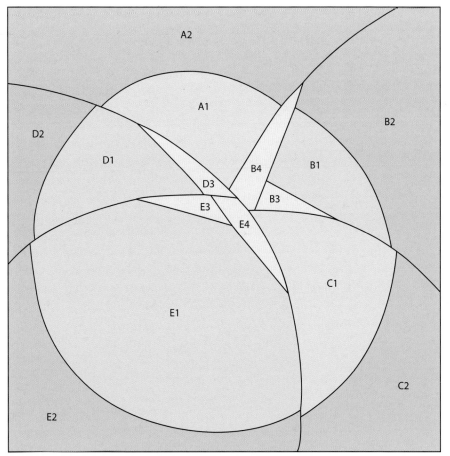

The size suggested is the minimum practical sewing size. To make it easier, make it bigger. During construction press the seam allowance in the direction indicated by the arrows on the piecing diagram.

Tomato curved-seam top view block
Enlarge this block 172% to an 8" x 8" square, see page 9.

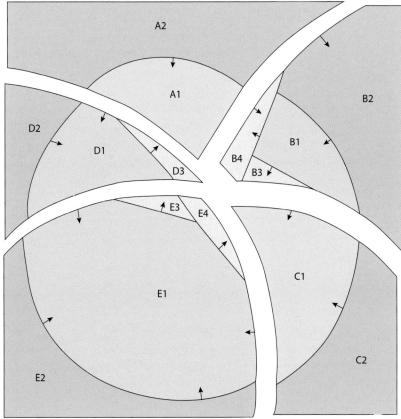

Sew:
A1 to A2
B1 to B2 to B3 to B4 to A
C1 to C2 to AB
D1 to D2 to D3
E1 to E2 to E3 to E4 to D to ABC

Tomato curved-seam top view piecing diagram

## ADDING SEPALS TO TOMATO WITH FOLDED FLAPS

Cut pieces B1, D1, E1 to extend all the way to the center of the tomato.

Mark placement lines for sepals. Sew B1 to B2, D1 to D2, E1 to E2.

Prepare folded strips to make sepals.

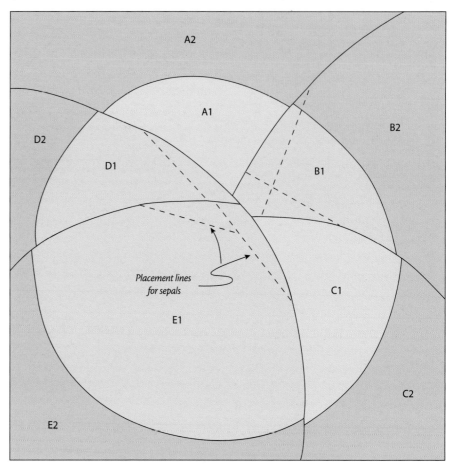

Tomato curved-seam top view block for folded sepals.
Enlarge this block 170% to an 8" x 8" square, see page 9.

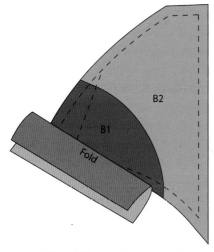

*1. Place fold on sepal placement line.*

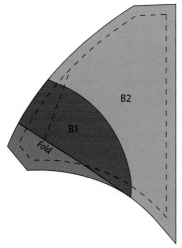

*2. Trim sepal to match
cut edge of B(1, 2).*

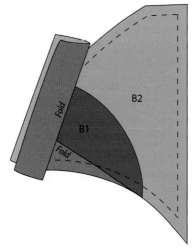

*3. Place fold for second sepal
on placement line.*

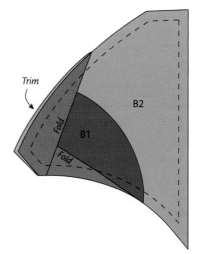

*4. Trim second sepal to
cut edge of B(1,2).*

*5. Sew above piece to A and to C
(folded edge can be left loose
or appliquéd down).*

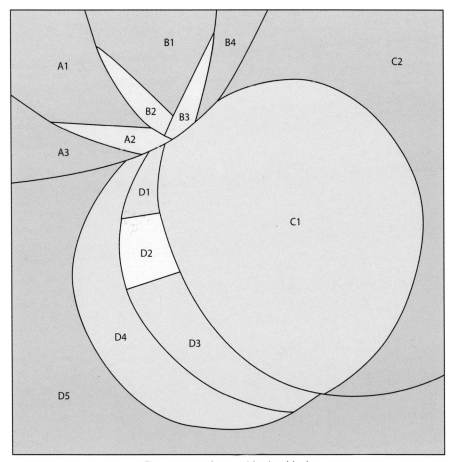

Tomato curved-seam side view block
Enlarge this block 172% to an 8" x 8" square, see page 9.

The size suggested is the minimum practical sewing size. To make it easier, make it bigger. During construction press the seam allowance in the direction indicated by the arrows on the piecing diagram.

If you can't find a fabric with a highlight in it for your tomato, you can add one in the piecing, D2 in this design.

Sew:
A1 to A2 to A3
B1 to B2 to B3 to B4 to A
C1 to C2
D1 to D2 to D3 to D4 to D5 to C to AB

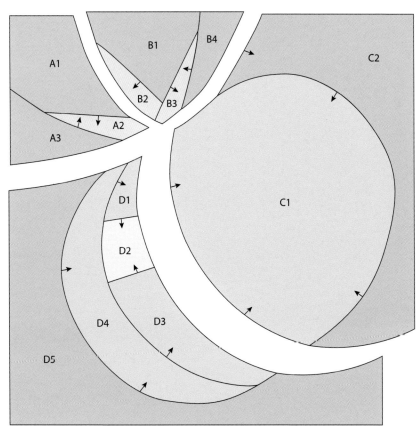

Tomato curved-seam side view piecing diagram

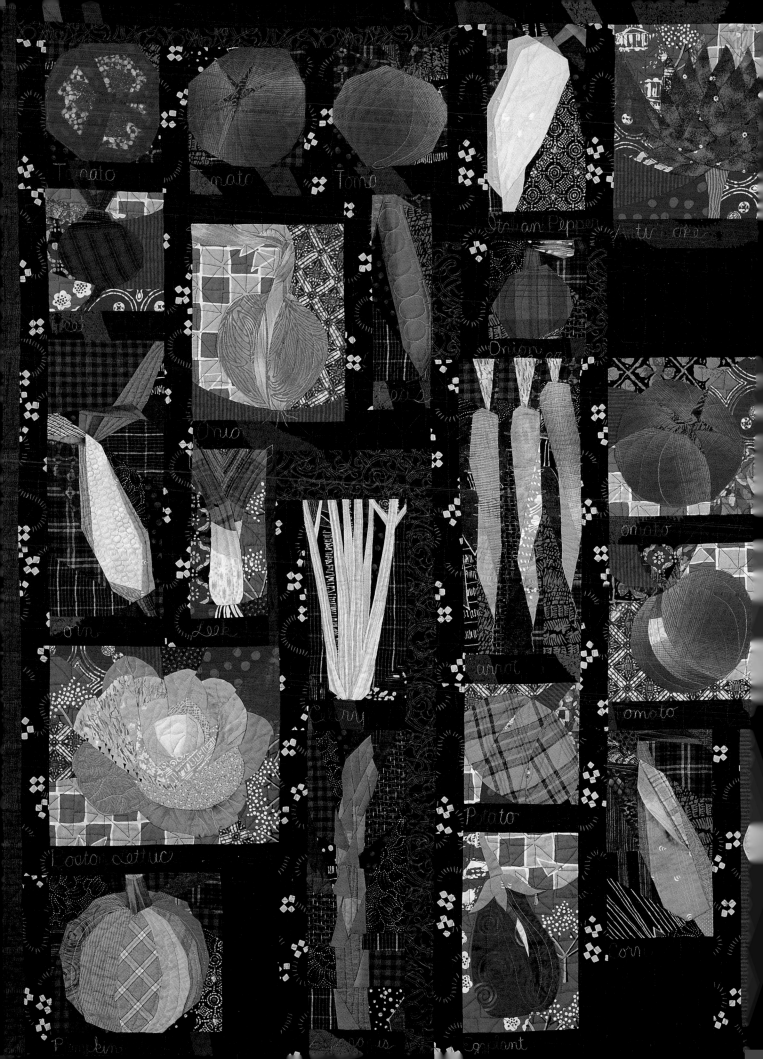

Sampler Quilt

I chose to make a sampler quilt, one of each of the blocks from this book, with the exception of the ristra block of which there are three. All of the blocks were sewn at the minimum recommended size. I first added a sashing strip to the left side and bottom of each block. The sashing strips finish 1½" wide (cut 2" wide).

I moved small paper blocks around on graph paper until I came up with this layout. I was trying to balance the colors in the quilt and fit the blocks together rather tightly. Rectangles were then added as needed between the

blocks. The bottom sashing strip of the straight-seam onion block was trimmed to 1" finished size (1½" cut) to make this layout work.

Drawing the entire plan on graph paper made it easier for me to calculate the sizes of the rectangles I would need to put the quilt together. The dimensions listed on the illustration are the finished size of each piece. Add ½" to each dimension for the cut size.

When I have time, I'm going to sew the other quilt designs I've drawn for the vegetables.

The sampler is charming as a quilt, but it doesn't do justice to the designs of the individual blocks.

The design of each block in this book has been planned not only to represent a vegetable, but also to make a design that will form an interesting larger pattern when repeated. The quilt designs I have chosen to illustrate as small drawings in each chapter are only a few of the many possible arrangements.

I hope you enjoy these vegetables. Best wishes and delicious quilting!

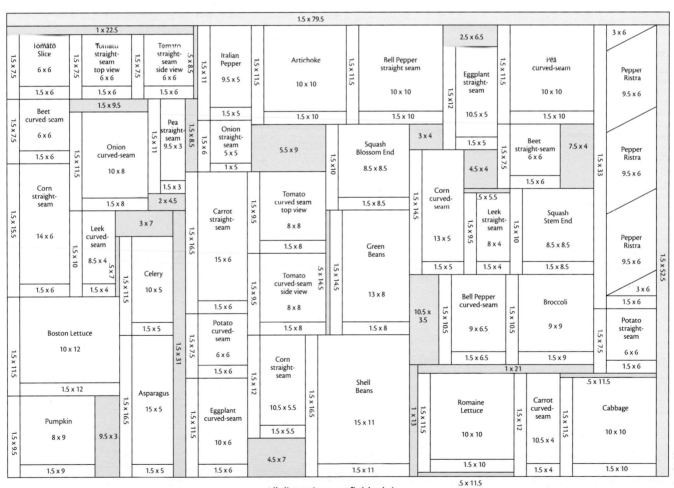

All dimensions are finished size.
Add ½" to each measurement when cutting each piece, i.e., for 1.5 x 9.5 cut 2 x 10.

## CONCLUSION

The blocks in this book have been designed with a number of principles I have developed in a long career of studying the pieced quilt medium. You will find a more complete discussion of this in *Piecing: Expanding the Basics*. This is the resource to use if you are interested in designing your own.

The layout of many of the small quilt drawings reflects my interest in symmetry patterning, laid out in detail in *Symmetry: A Design System for Quilters* (out of print). Those who have studied symmetry will find examples of P4, PG, P2GG, P4MG and several other symmetries in this book.

The vegetables have been selected because I like them. They also are a collection that represents many different shapes, textures, and colors. I've colored them here in a natural way. They could certainly be colored in any other vibrant hues you choose.

I love fabrics from many different sources, and am well known in the quilt world for using some unusual prints. You can see that here in the pieced sampler quilt. For more quilts using unusual fabrics, see *Art & Inspirations: Ruth B. McDowell* (out of print).

## OTHER BOOKS BY RUTH

*Symmetry: A Design System for Quiltmakers,*
Ruth B. McDowell, C & T Publishing,
Lafayette, CA, 1994 OUT OF PRINT

*Art & Inspirations: Ruth B. McDowell,*
C & T Publishing, Lafayette, CA,
1996 OUT OF PRINT

*Piecing: Expanding the Basics,*
Ruth B. McDowell,
C & T Publishing, Lafayette, CA,
1998 ISBN 1-57120-041-X

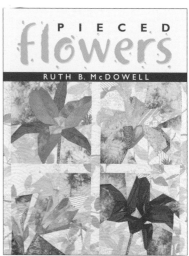

*Pieced Flowers,*
Ruth B. McDowell,
C & T Publishing, Lafayette, CA,
2000 ISBN 1-57120-091-6

## ABOUT THE AUTHOR

Ruth B. McDowell is an internationally known professional quilt artist, teacher, lecturer, and author. She has made over 300 quilts during the last two decades. Her quilts have been seen in many solo shows, as well as in dozens of magazines and books. Ruth resides in Winchester, Massachusetts.

Visit Ruth's web site at
**www.ruthbmcdowell.com**

For more information
write for a free catalog:
**C&T Publishing, Inc.**
P.O. Box 1456
Lafayette, CA 94549
(800) 284-1114
http://www.ctpub.com
email: ctinfo@ctpub.com

For Quilting supplies
**The Cotton Patch Mall Order**
3405 Brown Avenue, Dept. CTB
Lafayette, CA 94549
(800) 835-4418
(925) 283-7883
website: www.quiltusa.com
email: quiltusa@yahoo.com

# INDEX

## OTHER FINE BOOKS FROM C&T PUBLISHING:

*250 Continuous-Line Quilting Designs for Hand, Machine & Long-Arm Quilters,* Laura Lee Fritz

*Along the Garden Path: More Quilters and Their Gardens,* Jean Wells and Valorie Wells

*The Art of Classic Quiltmaking,* Harriet Hargrave and Sharyn Craig

*The Art of Machine Piecing: Quality Workmanship Through a Colorful Journey,* Sally Collins

*Block Magic: Over 50 Fun & Easy Blocks made from Squares and Rectangles,* Nancy Johnson-Srebro

*Color from the Heart: Seven Great Ways to Make Quilts with Colors You Love,* Gai Perry

*Color Play: Easy Steps to Imaginative Color in Quilts,* Joen Wolfrom

*Cotton Candy Quilts: Using Feedsacks, Vintage and Reproduction Fabrics,* Mary Mashuta

*Crazy Quilt Handbook, Revised 2nd Ed.,* Judith Baker Montano

*Curves in Motion: Quilt Designs & Techniques,* Judy B. Dales

*Cut-Loose Quilts: Stack, Slice, Switch & Sew,* Jan Mullen

*Do-It-Yourself Framed Quilts: Fast, Fun & Easy Projects,* Gai Perry

*Easy Pieces: Creative Color Play with Two Simple Blocks,* Margaret Miller

*Endless Possibilities: Using NO-FAIL Methods,* Nancy Johnson-Srebro

*Everything Flowers: Quilts from the Garden,* Jean and Valori Wells

*Fantastic Fabric Folding: Innovative Quilting Projects,* Rebecca Wat

*Flower Pounding: Quilt Projects for All Ages,* Amy Sandrin & Ann Frischkorn

*Free Stuff for Quilters on the Internet, 3rd Ed.,* Judy Heim and Gloria Hansen

*Free Stuff for Sewing Fanatics on the Internet,* Judy Heim and Gloria Hansen

*Free Stuff for Stitchers on the Internet,* Judy Heim and Gloria Hansen

*Free Stuff for Traveling Quilters on the Internet,* Gloria Hansen

*Free-Style Quilts: A "No Rules" Approach,* Susan Carlson

*From Fiber to Fabric: The Essential Guide to Quiltmaking Textiles,* Harriet Hargrave

*Ghost Layers & Color Washes: Three Steps to Spectacular Quilts,* Katie Pasquini Masopust

*Hand Appliqué with Alex Anderson: Seven Projects for Hand Appliqué,* Alex Anderson

*Hand Quilting with Alex Anderson: Six Projects for Hand Quilters,* Alex Anderson

*Heirloom Machine Quilting, Third Ed.,* Harriet Hargrave

*Kaleidoscopes & Quilts,* Paula Nadelstern

*Laurel Burch Quilts: Kindred Creatures,* Laurel Burch

*Lone Star Quilts and Beyond: Projects and Inspiration,* Jan Krentz

*Machine Embroidery and More: Ten Step-by-Step Projects Using Border Fabrics & Beads,* Kristen Dibbs

*Magical Four-Patch and Nine-Patch Quilts,* Yvonne Porcella

*Make Any Block Any Size,* Joen Wolfrom

*Mastering Quilt Marking: Marking Tools & Techniques, Choosing Stencils, Matching Borders & Corners,* Pepper Cory

*Measure the Possibilities with Omnigrid,* Nancy Johnson-Srebro

*The New England Quilt Museum Quilts: Featuring the Story of the Mill Girls, Instructions for 5 Heirloom Quilts,* Jennifer Gilbert

*On the Surface: Thread Embellishment & Fabric Manipulation,* Wendy Hill

*The Photo Transfer Handbook: Snap It, Print It, Stitch It!,* Jean Ray Laury

*Quilt Lovers Favorites,* American Patchwork & Quilting

*The Quilted Garden: Design & Make Nature-Inspired Quilts,* Jane A. Sassaman

*Quilted Memories: Celebrations of Life,* Mary Lou Weidman

*Quilting Back to Front: Fun & Easy No-Mark Techniques,* Larraine Scouler

*Quilting with Carol Armstrong: 30 Quilting Patterns, Appliqué Designs, 16 Projects,* Carol Armstrong

*Quilts for Guys: 15 Fun Projects For Your Favorite Fella*

*Setting Solutions,* Sharyn Craig

*Shadow Redwork with Alex Anderson: 24 Designs to Mix and Match,* Alex Anderson

*Skydyes: A Visual Guide to Fabric Painting,* Mickey Lawler

*Smashing Sets: Exciting Ways to Arrange Quilt Blocks,* Margaret J. Miller

*Snowflakes & Quilts,* Paula Nadelstern

*Stitch'n Flip Quilts: 14 Fantastic Projects,* Valori Wells

*Strips'n Curves: A New Spin on Strip Piecing,* Louisa Smith

*Through the Garden Gate: Quilters and Their Gardens,* Jean and Valori Wells

*Tradition with a Twist: Variations on Your Favorite Quilts,* Blanche Young & Dalene Young Stone

*Travels with Peaky and Spike: Doreen Speckmann's Quilting Adventures,* Doreen Speckmann

*Two-for-One Foundation Piecing: Reversible Quilts and More,* Wendy Hill

*The Visual Dance: Creating Spectacular Quilts,* Joen Wolfrom

*Wild Birds: Designs for Appliqué & Quilting,* Carol Armstrong

*Wildflowers: Designs for Appliqué & Quilting,* Carol Armstrong